Guide to Writing an Architecture-Oriented Sales Promotion Plan

-- SBC Architecture Description Language at Work --

William S. Chao

CONTENTS

- CONTENTS 3
- PREFACE 5
- ABOUT THE AUTHOR 7
- PART I: BASIC IDEAS 9
  - **Chapter 1: What Is a Plan?** 11
    - 1-1 Plan 11
      - 1-1-1 Product/Service 11
      - 1-1-2 Project Management 13
      - 1-1-3 Strategic Management 14
    - 1-2 Planning Chart 14
    - 1-3 Writing Down a Plan 15
  - **Chapter 2: What is a Sales Promotion Plan?** 19
    - 2-1 Sales Promotion Plan 19
    - 2-2 Sales Promotion Planning Chart 19
    - 2-3 Writing Down a Sales Promotion Plan 21
  - **Chapter 3: What is an Architecture-Oriented Sales Promotion Plan?** 23
    - 3-1 Architecture-Oriented Sales Promotion Plan 23
    - 3-2 Architecture-Oriented Sales Promotion Planning Chart 23
    - 3-3 Writing Down an Architecture-Oriented Sales Promotion Plan 25
  - **Chapter 4: Systems Theory 2.0** 27
    - 4-1 Introduction to System 27
      - 4-1-1 Systems Theory 1.0 Defining a System 28
      - 4-1-2 Physical and Conceptual Systems 30
      - 4-1-3 Boundary and Environment 32
      - 4-1-4 Evolution of a System 34
      - 4-1-5 High Order Systems 36
    - 4-2 Systems Structure and Systems Behavior 39
      - 4-2-1 Structure of Systems 39
      - 4-2-2 Behavior of Systems 41
    - 4-3 Structure-Behavior Coalescence 43
      - 4-3-1 Integrated Whole to Achieve the Systems Definition 43
      - 4-3-2 Integrating the Systems Structures and Systems Behaviors 44
      - 4-3-3 Structure-Behavior Coalescence to Facilitate an Integrated Whole 45
      - 4-3-4 Structure-Behavior Coalescence to Achieve the Systems Definition 45

    4-3-5 Systems Theory 2.0 Defining a System 46

PART II: SBC ARCHITECTURE DESCRIPTION LANGUAGE ..49

Chapter 5: Architecture Hierarchy Diagram 51
    5-1 Decomposition and Composition..51
    5-2 Multi-Level Decomposition and Composition 54
    5-3 Aggregated and Non-Aggregated Systems..............................56

Chapter 6: Framework Diagram 59
    6-1 Multi-Layer Decomposition and Composition 59
    6-2 Only Non-Aggregated Systems Appear in Framework Diagrams 60

Chapter 7: Component Operation Diagram.......................................63
    7-1 Operations of Each Component..63
    7-2 Drawing the Component Operation Diagram.........................66

Chapter 8: Component Connection Diagram....................................69
    8-1 Essence of a Connection 69
    8-2 Drawing the Component Connection Diagrams.....................71

Chapter 9: Structure-Behavior Coalescence Diagram 73
    9-1 Purpose of Structure-Behavior Coalescence Diagram............73
    9-2 Drawing the Structure-Behavior Coalescence Diagrams 74

Chapter 10: Interaction Flow Diagram...77
    10-1 Individual Behavior Represented by Interaction Flow Diagram 77
    10-2 Drawing the Interaction Flow Diagrams 78

PART III: CASE STUDIES 83

Chapter 11: Convenience Store's Get 2nd 50% off Sales Promotion Plan ..85
    11-1 Architecture-Oriented Convenience Store's Get 2nd 50% off Sales Promotion Planning Chart..85
    11-2 Writing Down an Architecture-Oriented Convenience Store's Get 2nd 50% off Sales Promotion Plan 86

Chapter 12: Department Store's Car Sweepstakes Sales Promotion Plan ...99
    12-1 Architecture-Oriented Department Store's Car Sweepstakes Sales Promotion Planning Chart..99
    12-2 Writing Down an Architecture-Oriented Department Store's Car Sweepstakes Sales Promotion Plan 100

APPENDIX: SBC ARCHITECTURE DESCRIPTION LANGUAGE
....111

PREFACE

No matter which type of planning, when we start to develop it, the most important issue is to seize the most relevant task to this planning. The task of a plan can be simple or complex. Whether simple or complex, planning task must include the following three major elements: (B) Product/Service, (C) Project Management and (D) Strategic Management.

Because product/service plays an innermost ring role in the planning, so it is surely the most important one. In other words, if the innermost "Product/Service" is not clearly described then neither the second inner "Project Management" nor the outermost "Strategic Management" will be clearly described.

Therefore, the key to writing a good "sales promotion plan" lies in a clear description of the innermost "sales promotion system". This book uses the SBC architecture description language to accomplish the description of the "sales promotion system". No SBC architecture means no planning. By reading this "Guide to Writing an Architecture-Oriented Sales Promotion Plan" book, readers shall find that SBC architecture truly helps us write an excellent Sales Promotion Plan in a tremendously effective and efficient way.

ABOUT THE AUTHOR

Dr. William S. Chao is the CEO & founder of SBC Architecture International®. SBC (Structure-Behavior Coalescence) architecture is a systems architecture which demands the integration of systems structure and systems behavior of a system. SBC architecture applies to hardware architecture, software architecture, enterprise architecture, knowledge architecture and thinking architecture. The core theme of SBC architecture is: "Architecture = Structure + Behavior."

William S. Chao received his bachelor degree (1976) in telecommunication engineering and master degree (1981) in information engineering, both from the National Chiao-Tung University, Taiwan. From 1976 till 1983, he worked as an engineer at Chung-Hwa Telecommunication Company, Taiwan.

William S. Chao received his master degree (1985) in information science and Ph.D. degree (1988) in information science, both from the University of Alabama at Birmingham, USA. From 1988 till 1991, he worked as a computer scientist at GE Research and Development Center, Schenectady, New York, USA.

Dr. William S. Chao has been teaching at National Sun Yat-Sen University, Taiwan since 1992 and now serves as the president of Association of Enterprise Architects, Taiwan Chapter. His research covers: systems architecture, hardware architecture, software architecture, enterprise architecture, knowledge architecture and thinking architecture.

8

PART I: BASIC IDEAS

Chapter 1: What Is a Plan?

This chapter describes what a plan or planning is. First, we have to understand the major elements of a plan. After that, we shall draw the planning chart based on those major elements. Finally we will be, according to the planning chart, writing down a plan in detail.

1-1 Plan

A plan or planning can be roughly divided into the following types: (01) Advertising Planning, (02) Internal Improvement Planning, (03) Event Planning, (04) Business Planning, (05) New Product Development Planning, (06) Opening a Store Planning , (07) Chain Stores Development Planning, (08) Questionnaire Planning, (09) Animation Planning, (10) Digital Game Planning, (11) Multimedia Planning, (12) Procurement Planning, (13) Innovative Services Planning, (14) Scientific Project Planning, (15) Multimedia Marketing Planning, (16) Marketing Planning, (17) Sales Promotion Planning, and so on.

No matter which type of planning, when we start to develop it, the most important issue is to seize the most relevant task to this planning. The task of a plan can be simple or complex. Whether simple or complex, planning task must include the following three major elements: (B) Product/Service, (C) Project Management and (D) Strategic Management.

1-1-1 Product/Service

Product or service is the tangible and deliverable objectives of this planning, the resulting "ultimate product/service". The planning outcome objective may be a product or service system. For this "product/service," if we can describe it more specific, the more beneficial it will be for planning. Different planning types have different "product/service," as shown in Figure 1-1.

Types of Plan	Product/Service
Advertising Planning	Advertisement
Internal Improvement Planning	Organization
Event Planning	Activity
Business Planning	Business System
New Product Development Planning	Product
Opening a Store Planning	Shop
Chain Stores Development Planning	Chain Stores
Questionnaire Planning	Questionnaire
Animation Planning	Animation
Digital Game Planning	Digital Game
Multimedia Planning	Multimedia
Procurement planning	Procurement System
Innovative Services Planning	Service System
Scientific Project Planning	Scientific Project System
Multimedia Marketing Planning	Multimedia Marketing System
Marketing Planning	Marketing System
Sales Promotion Planning	Sales Promotion System

Figure 1-1   Product/Service for Different Types of Plan

For advertising planning, its product/service is the presentation of the "advertisement" or "multimedia advertisement" that customers watch in the newspaper or on television. For internal improvement planning, its product/service is the transformation of the "organization" which the general manager or boss wants to see. For event planning, its product/service is the presentation of the "activities" which customers may participate. For business planning, its product/service is the presentation of the "business system" in which a manager manages and an operator operates. For new product development planning, its product/service is the presentation of the "commodity" which the customers will be interested in buying. For opening a store planning, its product/service is the presentation of the new "shop" where guests can enjoy their shopping. For chain stores development planning, its product/service is the presentation of the "chain store" where goods can circulate. For questionnaire planning, its product/service is the presentation of the "questionnaire" which will be filled. For animation planning, its product/service is the presentation of the "animation" watched by the audience. For digital game planning, its product/service is the presentation of the "digital game" engaged by the players. For multimedia planning, its product/service is the presentation of the "multimedia" viewed by the audience. For procurement planning, its product/service is the presentation of the "procurement system" in which a buyer operates. For innovative services planning, its product/service is the presentation of the new "service system" which a company provides to its customers. For scientific project planning, its product/service is the presentation of the "scientific project system" which is developed by a company or a consortium of legal entities. For multimedia marketing planning, its product/service is the presentation of the "multimedia marketing system" which a company may adopt to execute. For marketing planning, its product/service is the presentation of the "marketing system" which a company may adopt to execute. For sales promotion planning, its product/service is the presentation of the "sales promotion system" which a company may use for its sales practices.

1-1-2 Project Management

Project management is the extra handling of the work, for the planning to complete the product/service. The extra handling of the work includes: (C01) Time Schedule and (C02) Cost Estimation, etc.

The time schedule of a plan is very important. Time plays a significant factor in the success of the pursuit of planning, sometimes clear and sometimes fuzzy. When setting the result we want to achieve, we should indicate the specific time schedule when we can show the results. In other words, whenever planning to achieve the intended results, the time schedule must be clearly specified.

No one wants to do business at a loss. The same principle applies to a plan. No boss will show any interests if it is a losing money plan. Therefore, all planning-related estimation of costs, expenses, income, and so must be stated clearly so a boss would have sufficient information to approve or disapprove the plan.

1-1-3 Strategic Management

Strategic management is the strategic thinking, for the planning to complete the product/service. With the strategic thinking, so we can understand the feasibility of the plan. In other words, we shall consider strategically about the plan on: (D01) Goal Drivers, (D02) Goal Assumptions, (D03) Goal Constraints and (D04) SWOT (Strengths, Weaknesses, Opportunities, Threat) Analysis, etc.

Goal drivers are up from the policy considerations, the goal driver is kind of how we got to be this prompted planning. Goal assumptions are taking into account of those assumptions that have a positive impact on this planning. Goal constraints are up from the policy considerations, the goal constraints are related to those restrictions which have a negative impact on this planning. SWOT (Strengths, Weaknesses, Opportunities, Threat) analysis is to analyze the internal strengths, weaknesses, opportunities and threats, and so for executing this plan.

1-2 Planning Chart

We use a chart to display the three major elements of a plan as shown in Figure 1-2. The planning chart, like a mandala, can be interpreted as gradually extending outward from the innermost ring, can also be interpreted as an external gradually move closer to the innermost ring.

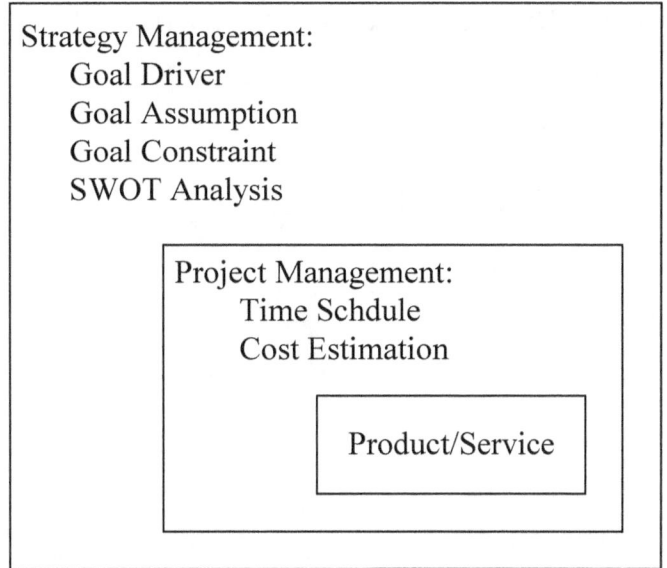

Figure 1-2   Planning Chart

There are three rings in the planning chart. The innermost ring is: (B) Product/Service; second inner ring is the project management which includes: (C01) Time Schedule and (C02) Cost Estimation; outermost ring is the strategic management which includes: (D01) Goal Drivers, (D02) Goal Assumptions, (D03) Goal Constraints and (D04) SWOT Analysis. Project management is around the "product/service". That is to say, project management is in line with the "product/service". Strategic management is around the "project management" and "product/service". That is to say, strategic management is in line with the "project management" and "product/service".

Because product/service plays an innermost ring role in the planning chart, so it is surely the most important one. In other words, if the innermost "product/service" is not clearly described then neither the second inner project management which includes: (C01) Time Schedule and (C02) Cost Estimation, nor the outermost strategic management which includes: (D01) Goal Drivers, (D02) Goal Assumptions, (D03) Goal Constraints and (D04) SWOT Analysis, will be clearly described.

1-3 Writing Down a Plan

With the planning chart, we are able to write down a plan. Basically, the writing of a plan follows the planning chart: (A01) Title and Cover, (A02) Contents, (A03) Planning Team Members, (A04) Planning Purposes, (B) Planning Objectives

(Product/Service), (C01) Time Schedule, (C02) Cost Estimation, (D01) Goal Drivers, (D02) Goal Assumptions, (D03) Goal Constraints and (D04) SWOT Analysis, as shown in Figure 1-3.

Plan

Title and Cover

Table of Contents
****

Planning Team Members
****

Planning Purposes
****

Planning Objectives (Product/Service)
****

Time Schedule
****

Cost Estimation
****

Goal Drivers
****

Goal Assumptions
****

Goal Constraints
****

SWOT Analysis
****

Figure 1-3   Writing of a Plan

Chapter 2: What is a Sales Promotion Plan?

This chapter explains what a sales promotion plan is. First, we will introduce that the sales promotion plan belongs to one of many planning types. After that, we shall introduce the sales promotion planning chart. Finally we will be, according to the sales promotion planning chart, writing down a sales promotion plan in detail.

2-1 Sales Promotion Plan

A plan or planning can be roughly divided into the following types: (01) Advertising Planning, (02) Internal Improvement Planning, (03) Event Planning, (04) Business Planning, (05) New Product Development Planning, (06) Opening a Store Planning , (07) Chain Stores Development Planning, (08) Questionnaire Planning, (09) Animation Planning, (10) Digital Game Planning, (11) Multimedia Planning, (12) Procurement Planning, (13) Innovative Services Planning, (14) Scientific Project Planning, (15) Multimedia Marketing Planning, (16) Marketing Planning, (17) Sales Promotion Planning, and so on.

Sales promotion plan belongs to one of many planning types listed above. We use the sales promotion planning chart to completely represent the feature of a sales promotion plan.

2-2 Sales Promotion Planning Chart

Among the many kinds of planning types, each type has a corresponding planning chart. If we say that the sales promotion plan is one of many kinds of planning types, then the sales promotion planning chart is one of many kinds of planning charts.

According to the above description, we will draw the sales promotion planning chart shown in Figure 2-1. The sales promotion planning chart, like a mandala, can be interpreted as gradually extending outward from the innermost ring, can also be interpreted as an external gradually move closer to the innermost ring. There are three rings in the sales promotion planning chart. The innermost ring is: (B) Sales Promotion System; second inner ring is the project management which includes: (C01) Time Schedule and (C02) Cost Estimation; outermost ring is the strategic management which includes: (D01) Goal Drivers, (D02) Goal Assumptions, (D03) Goal Constraints and (D04) SWOT Analysis. Project management is around the "sales promotion system". That is to say, project management is in line with the "sales promotion system". Strategic management is around the "project management" and "sales promotion system". That is to say, strategic management is in line with the "project management" and "sales promotion system".

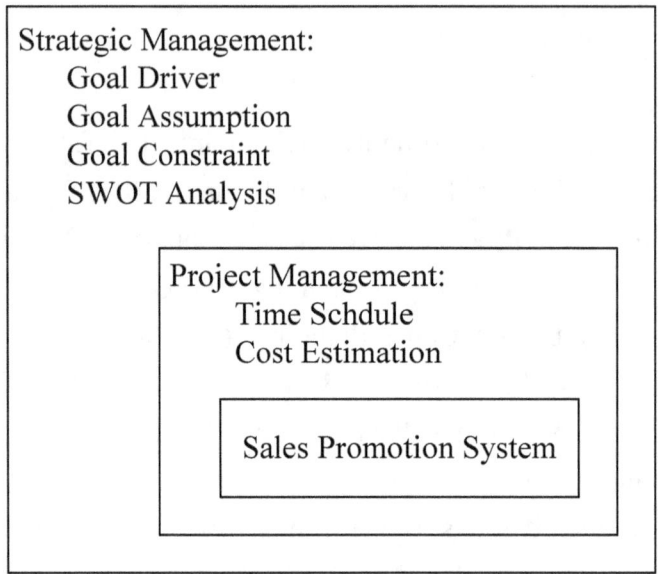

Figure 2-1   Sales Promotion Planning Chart

Comparing the sales promotion planning chart with the planning chart discussed in the previous chapter, the difference between them is that the innermost ring of the planning chart is generic "product/service," and the innermost ring of the sales promotion planning chart is a dedicated "sales promotion system". As sales promotion planning has a specific objective, so its "product/service" must also be changed to a dedicated objective, that is, "sales promotion system".

Because sales promotion system plays an innermost ring role in the sales promotion planning chart, so it is surely the most important one. In other words, if the innermost "sales promotion system" is not clearly described then neither the second inner project management which includes: (C01) Time Schedule and (C02) Cost Estimation, nor the outermost strategic management which includes: (D01) Goal Drivers, (D02) Goal Assumptions, (D03) Goal Constraints and (D04) SWOT Analysis, will be clearly described.

2-3 Writing Down a Sales Promotion Plan

With the sales promotion planning chart, we are able to write down a sales promotion plan. Basically, the writing of a sales promotion plan follows the sales promotion planning chart: (A01) Title and Cover, (A02) Contents, (A03) Planning Team Members, (A04) Planning Purposes, (B) Planning Objectives (Sales Promotion System), (C01) Time Schedule, (C02) Cost Estimation, (D01) Goal Drivers, (D02) Goal Assumptions, (D03) Goal Constraints and (D04) SWOT Analysis, as shown in Figure 2-2.

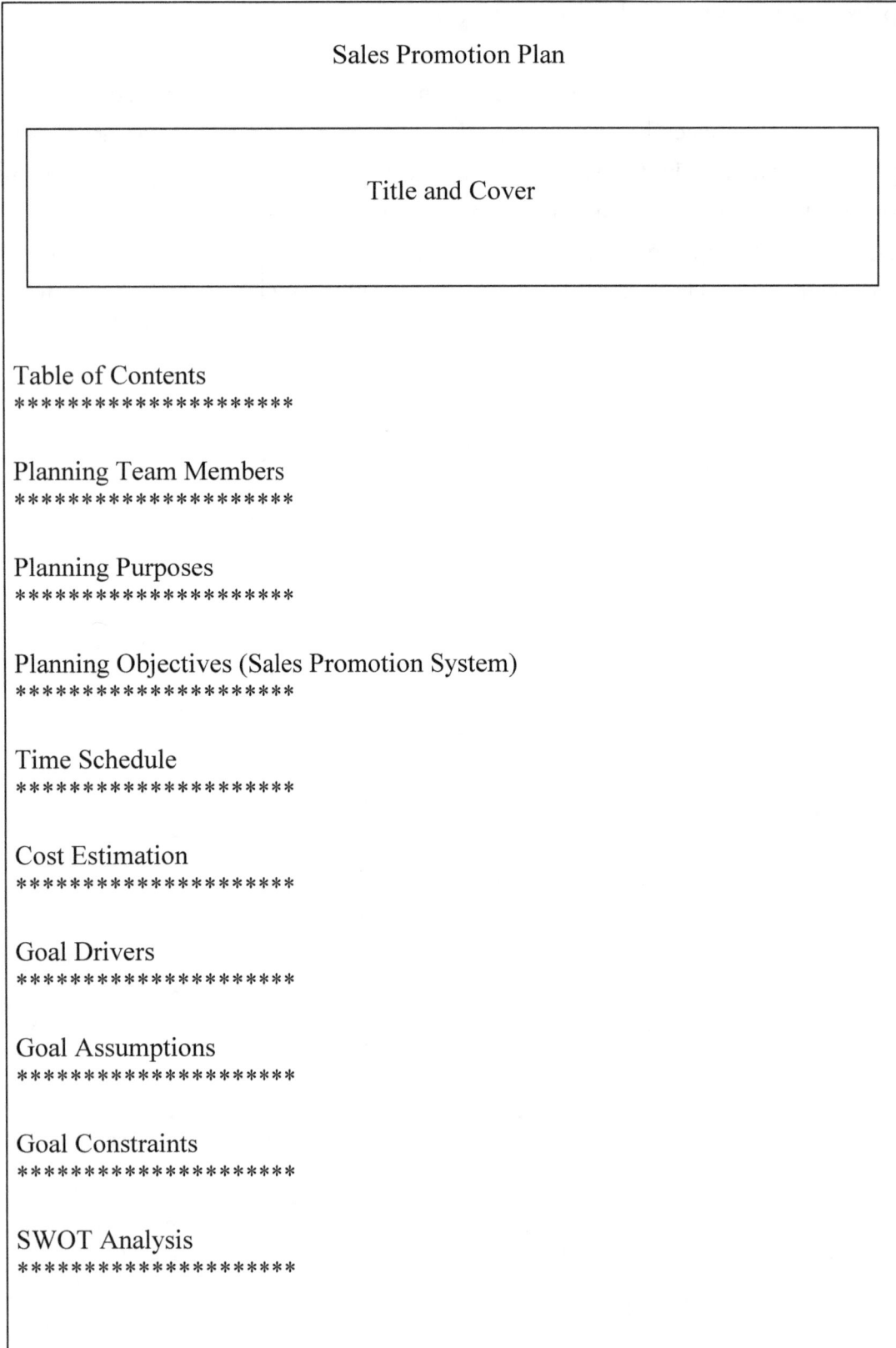

Figure 2-2　Writing of a Sales Promotion Plan

Chapter 3: What is an Architecture-Oriented Sales Promotion Plan?

This chapter explains what an architecture-oriented sales promotion plan is. First, we will introduce that the architecture-oriented sales promotion plan belongs to one methodology of many sales promotion planning methods. After that, we shall introduce the architecture-oriented sales promotion planning chart. Finally we will be, according to the architecture-oriented sales promotion planning chart, writing down an architecture-oriented sales promotion plan in detail.

3-1 Architecture-Oriented Sales Promotion Plan

Sales promotion planning methods can be divided into roughly the following types: (01) Process-Oriented Sales Promotion Planning Methods, (02) Function-Oriented Sales Promotion Planning Methods, (03) Structure-Oriented Sales Promotion Planning Methods, (04) Object-Oriented Sales Promotion Planning Methods, (05) Architecture-Oriented Sales Promotion Planning Methods, etc.

Architecture-oriented sales promotion planning method belongs to one of many sales promotion planning types listed above. We use the architecture-oriented sales promotion planning chart to completely represent the feature of an architecture-oriented sales promotion plan.

3-2 Architecture-Oriented Sales Promotion Planning Chart

Among the many kinds of sales promotion planning methods, each method has a corresponding sales promotion planning chart. If we say that the architecture-oriented sales promotion plan is one of many kinds of sales promotion planning methods, then the architecture-oriented sales promotion planning chart is one of many kinds of sales promotion planning charts.

According to the above description, we will draw the architecture-oriented sales promotion planning chart shown in Figure 3-1. The sales architecture-oriented promotion planning chart, like a mandala, can be interpreted as gradually extending outward from the innermost ring, can also be interpreted as an external gradually move closer to the innermost ring. There are three rings in the architecture-oriented sales promotion planning chart. The innermost ring is: (B) SBC Architecture of Sales Promotion System; second inner is the project management which includes: (C01) Time Schedule and (C02) Cost Estimation; outermost ring is the strategic management which includes: (D01) Goal Drivers, (D02) Goal Assumptions, (D03) Goal Constraints and (D04) SWOT Analysis. Project management is around the "SBC architecture of sales promotion system". That is to say, project management is in line with the "SBC architecture of sales promotion system". Strategic management is around the "project management" and "SBC architecture of sales promotion system". That is to say, strategic management is in line with the "project management" and "SBC architecture of sales promotion system".

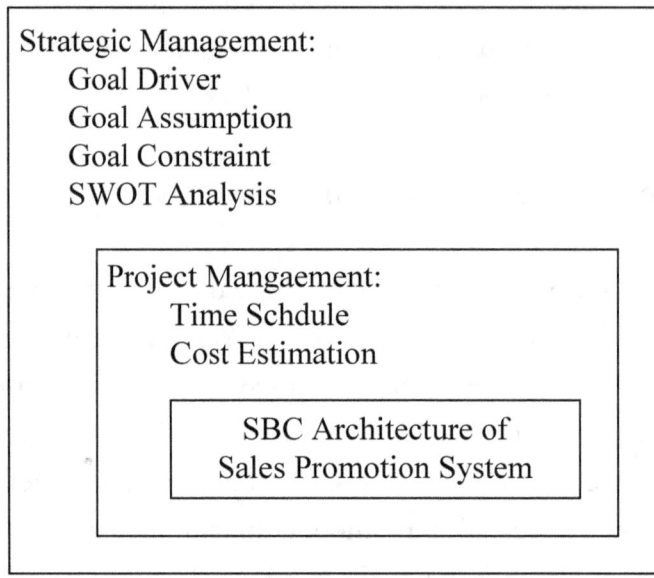

Figure 3-1　Architecture-Oriented Sales Promotion Planning Chart

Comparing the architecture-oriented sales promotion planning chart with the sales promotion planning chart discussed in the previous chapter, the difference between them is that the innermost ring of the sales promotion planning chart is "sales promotion system," and the innermost ring of the architecture-oriented sales promotion planning chart is a dedicated "SBC architecture of sales promotion system". As architecture-oriented sales promotion planning has a specific objective, so its "sales promotion system" must also be changed to a dedicated objective, that is, "SBC architecture of sales promotion system".

Because SBC architecture of sales promotion system plays an innermost ring role in the architecture-oriented sales promotion planning chart, so it is surely the most important one. In other words, if the innermost "SBC architecture of sales promotion system" is not clearly described then neither the second inner project management which includes: (C01) time schedule and (C02) cost estimation, nor the outermost strategic management which includes: (D01) goal drivers, (D02) goal assumptions, (D03) goal constraints and (D04) SWOT analysis, will be clearly described.

The special of this book lies in this "SBC architecture of sales promotion system". If the innermost (B) SBC architecture of sales promotion system is clearly described then either the second inner project management which includes: (C01) Time Schedule and (C02) Cost Estimation, or the outermost strategic management which includes: (D01) Goal Drivers, (D02) Goal Assumptions, (D03) Goal Constraints and (D04) SWOT Analysis, are likely to be clearly described. Conversely, if the innermost (B) SBC architecture of sales promotion system is not clearly described then neither the second inner project management which includes: (C01) Time Schedule and (C02) Cost Estimation, nor the outermost strategic management which includes: (D01) Goal Drivers, (D02) Goal Assumptions, (D03) Goal Constraints and (D04) SWOT Analysis, will be clearly described.

For "SBC architecture of sales promotion system" to be clearly described, we must fully use the mechanism of systems theory 2.0 (architectural theory) mentioned in this book. Systems theory 2.0 adopts the SBC architecture description language (SBC-ADL) to complete the definition of a system, so it can 100% clearly describe the "SBC architecture of sales promotion system".

3-3 Writing Down an Architecture-Oriented Sales Promotion Plan

With the architecture-oriented sales promotion planning chart, we are able to write down an architecture-oriented sales promotion plan.

Basically, an architecture-oriented sales promotion plan follows: (A01) Title and Cover, (A02) Contents, (A03) Planning Team Members, (A04) Planning Purposes, (B) Planning Objectives (SBC Architecture of Sales Promotion System), (C01) Time Schedule, (C02) Cost Estimation, (D01) Goal Drivers, (D02) Goal Assumptions, (D03) Goal Constraints and (D04) SWOT Analysis, as shown in Figure 3-2.

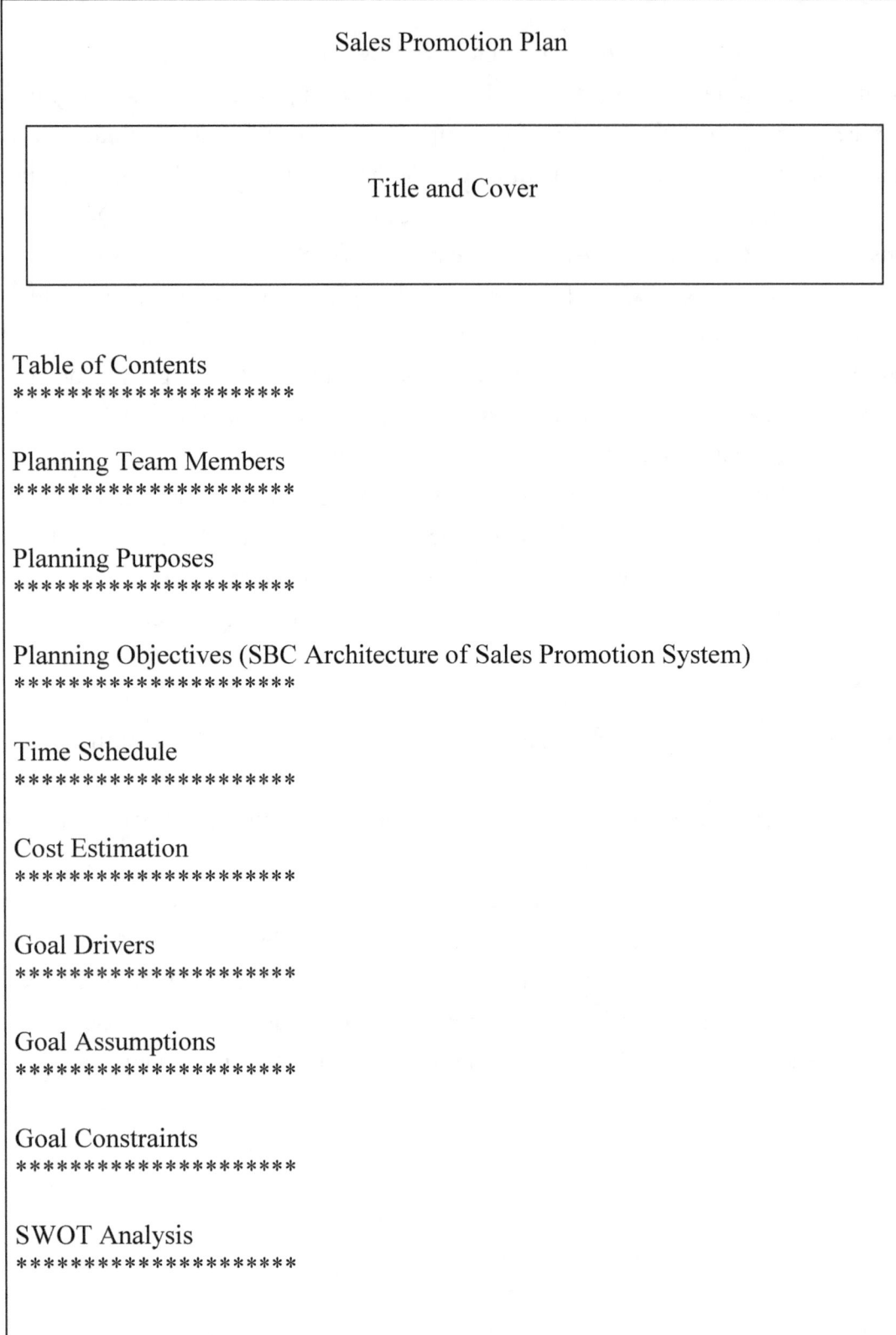

Figure 3-2   Architecture-Oriented Sales Promotion Plan

Chapter 4: Systems Theory 2.0

Human beings have employed the concept of systems so widely in all kinds of scientific studies. A systems definition is used to describe what a system is. A system has been defined, by systems theory 1.0, hopefully to be an integrated whole, embodied in its assembled components, their interrelationships with each other and the environment. This systems theory 1.0 defining a system possesses one cardinal deficiency. The deficiency comes from that it does not describe the integration of systems structure and systems behavior.

Systems structure and systems behavior are the two most significant views of a system. In order to achieve a truly integrated whole of a system, we first need to integrate the systems structure and behavior together. In other words, integration of the systems structure and systems behavior results in the integration of a whole system. Since systems theory 1.0 does not describe the integration of systems structure and systems behavior, very likely it only hopes and will never be able to really form an integrated whole of a system. In this situation, systems theory 1.0 is incompetent in defining a system.

Structure-behavior coalescence (SBC) provides a sophisticated way to integrate the structure and behavior of a system. A system is therefore redefined, by systems theory 2.0 (architectural theory), truly to be an integrated whole through the structure-behavior coalescence, embodied in its assembled components, their interactions (or handshakes) with each other and the environment. Systems theory 2.0 adopts the SBC architecture description language (SBC-ADL) to formally define the essence of a system and its details at the same time. The SBC-ADL contains six fundamental diagrams: a) architecture hierarchy diagram, b) framework diagram, c) component operation diagram, d) component connection diagram, e) structure-behavior coalescence diagram and f) interaction flow diagram. Since Systems theory 2.0 (Architectural theory) describes the integration of systems structure and systems behavior, definitely it is able to form an integrated whole of a system. In this situation, systems theory 2.0 is fully capable of defining a system.

This chapter delineates the systems theory 2.0 based on the SBC-ADL. By introduction and elaboration of the SBC-ADL, we will understand clearly how the systems theory 2.0 helps us truly define an integrated whole of a system.

4-1 Introduction to System

The word "system" originates from the Greek term, systēma, meaning "composition" or "whole". The concept of systems has been so widely used in all kinds of scientific studies such as systems analysis and design, systems architecting, systems architecture, systems bible, systems biology, system dynamics, systems ecology, systems engineering, systems medicine, systems modeling, systems physiology, systems requirement, systems science, systems theory, systems thinking, systems view.

4-1-1 Systems Theory 1.0 Defining a System

All things that strike us as something independent are essentially parts of a system. We usually call the parts of a system its components. Every system is something the whole. Systems emphasize the holistic vision.

The need for systems definition arises because any real-life system is inherently complicated. It is impossible to comprehend fully the intricate interrelationships of any system of the real world with its environment, or to describe all its components and each of its details. Systems definition is an artifact created by humans to describe what a system is.

Systems theory 1.0 defines a system, as shown in Figure 4-1, hopefully to be an integrated whole, embodied in its assembled components, their interrelationships with each other and the environment.

> A system, hopefully is an integrated whole,
> embodied in its assembled components,
> their interrelationships with each other and the environment.

Figure 4-1   Systems Theory 1.0 Defining a System

Components are sometimes labeled as parts, entities, objects, building blocks and non-aggregated systems. Interrelated components make a system not only a whole but also hopefully an integrated whole.

A system defined by the systems theory 1.0 has the following characteristics: 1) hopefully, it is an integrated whole; 2) it is embodied in its assembled components; and 3) components are interrelated with each other and the environment.

A systems definition is used to describe what a system is. Without a systems definition, everybody has his own saying about a system and never be able to reach a consensus. For example, Bruce Kennedy thinks the *Classroom_4069* is embodied in its assembled components of *desk_1* and *chair_1*, their interrelationships with each other and the environment; Tom Johnson thinks the *Classroom_4069* is embodied in its assembled components of *desk_1*, *chair_1*, *chair_2* and *chair_3*, their interrelationships with each other and the environment. It is impossible for Bruce Kennedy and Tom Johnson to work together on the *Classroom_4069* if can not reach a common definition.

To solve the conflict between Bruce Kennedy and Tom Johnson, here comes the systems theory 1.0 defining the *Classroom_4069*, as shown in Figure 4-2, hopefully to be an integrated whole, embodied in its assembled components of *desk_1*, *chair_1* and *chair_2*, their interrelationships with each other and the environment.

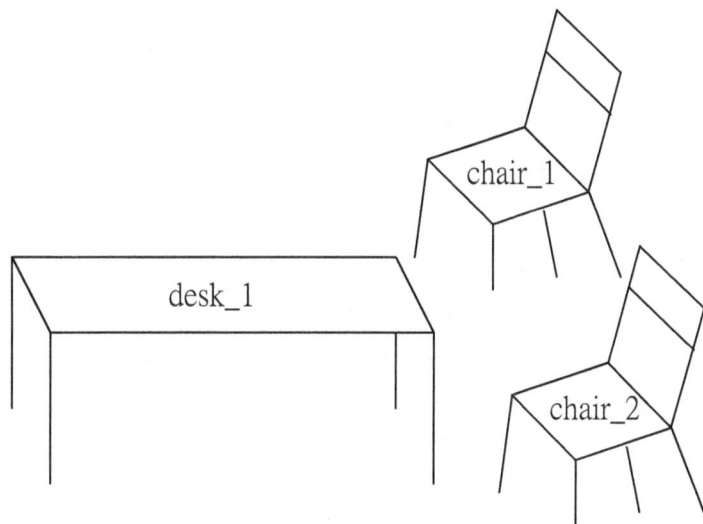

Figure 4-2   Systems Theory 1.0 Defining the *Classroom_4069*

As a second example, the systems theory 1.0 defines a *bicycle*, as shown in Figure 4-3, hopefully to be an integrated whole, embodied in its assembled components of *wheels*, *frame* and *pedal*, their interrelationships with each other and the environment.

Figure 4-3   Systems Theory 1.0 Defining a *Bicycle*

As the third example, the systems theory 1.0 defines a *swing*, as shown in Figure 4-4, hopefully to be an integrated whole, embodied in its assembled components of *ropes* and *seat*, their interrelationships with each other and the environment.

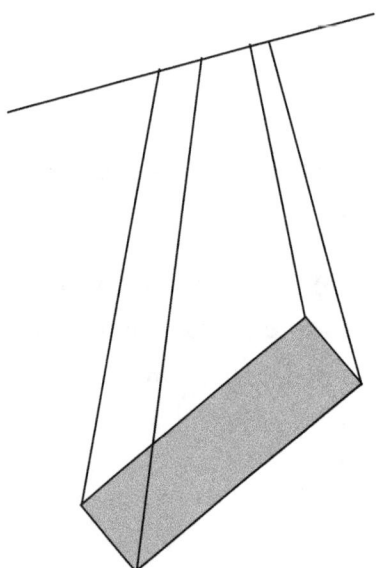

Figure 4-4   Systems Theory 1.0 Defining a *Swing*

4-1-2 Physical and Conceptual Systems

In general, the systems are divided into two categories: 1) physical systems and 2) conceptual systems.

A physical system exists in the physical world. A physical system is also called a concrete or real system. For example, a *telephone* composed of *microphone*, *earphone* and *keypad*, shown in Figure 4-5, is a physical, concrete, or real system.

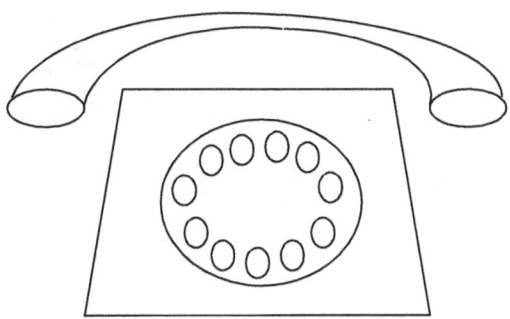

Figure 4-5   A Telephone is a Physical System

As a second example, a *stool* composed of *seat* and *legs*, shown in Figure 4-6, is a physical, concrete, or real system.

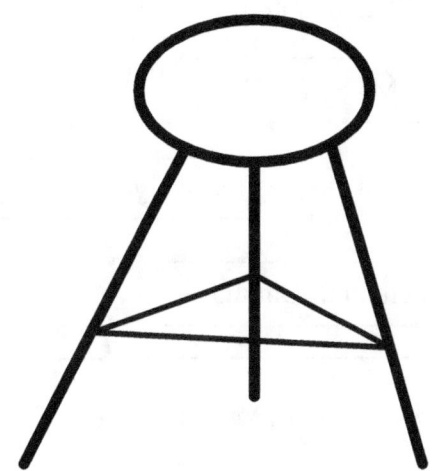

Figure 4-6   A Stool is a Physical System

A conceptual system is a system that is composed of non-physical components, i.e., ideas, thoughts, or concepts. A conceptual system exists in the conceptual, abstract, or virtual world. For example, the "*Snow White and the Seven Dwarfs*" fairy tale composed of the "*snow white*" princess and the *seven dwarfs*, shown in Figure 4-7, is a conceptual or virtual system.

Figure 4-7 *Snow White and the Seven Dwarfs* is a Conceptual System

As a second example, For example, the "*Multi-Tier Personal Data System*" software composed of *MTPDS_GUI*, *Age_Logic*, *Overweight_Logic* and *Personal_Database*, shown in Figure 4-8, is a conceptual or virtual system.

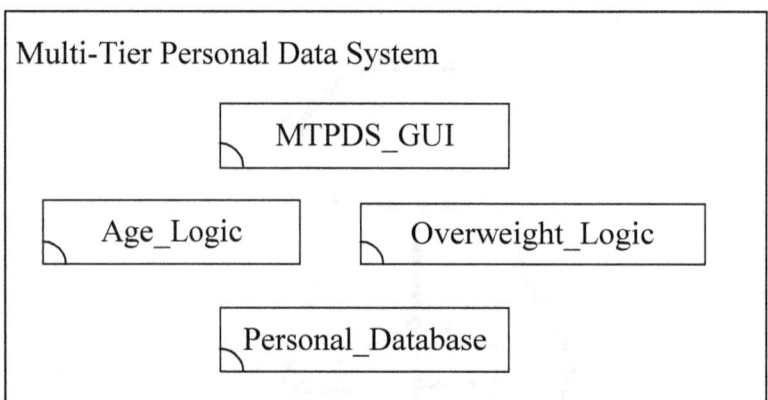

Figure 4-8 *Multi-Tier Personal Data System* is a Conceptual System

4-1-3 Boundary and Environment

We scope a system by defining its boundary as shown in Figure 4-9. All components of the system are inside the boundary while the environment is outside the boundary.

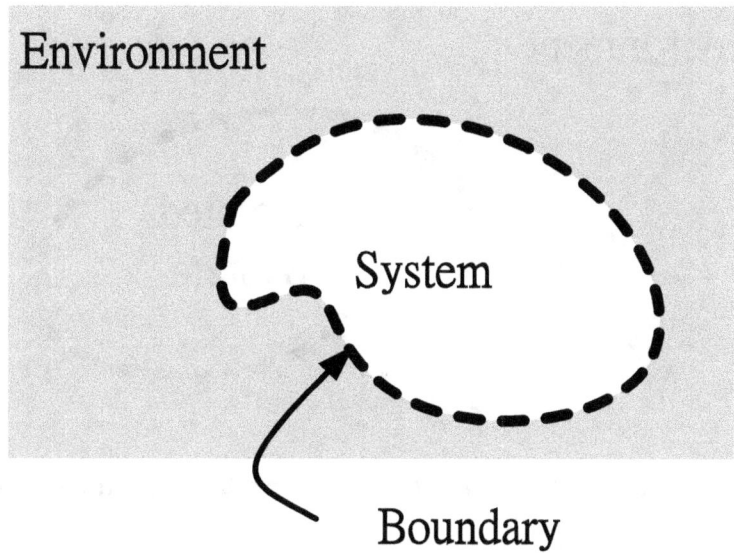

Figure 4-9   Boundary and Environment of a System

The environment is also known as the surroundings. A system may or may not interrelate with the environment. An open system interrelates with the environment through the exchange of matter, energy, data, information, or message as shown in Figure 4-10.

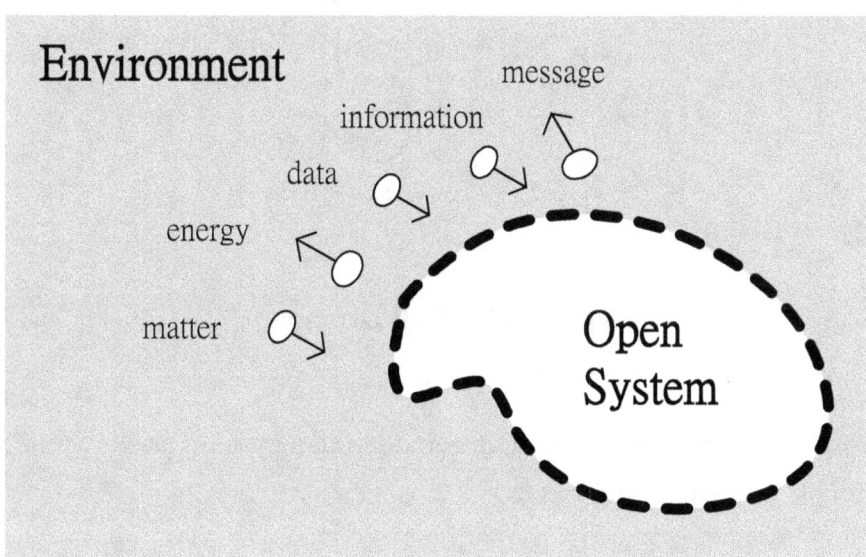

Figure 4-10   Open System Interrelates with the Environment

An isolated system does not interrelate with the environment at all. There is no exchange of matter, energy, data, information, or message between the isolated system and the environment as shown in Figure 4-11.

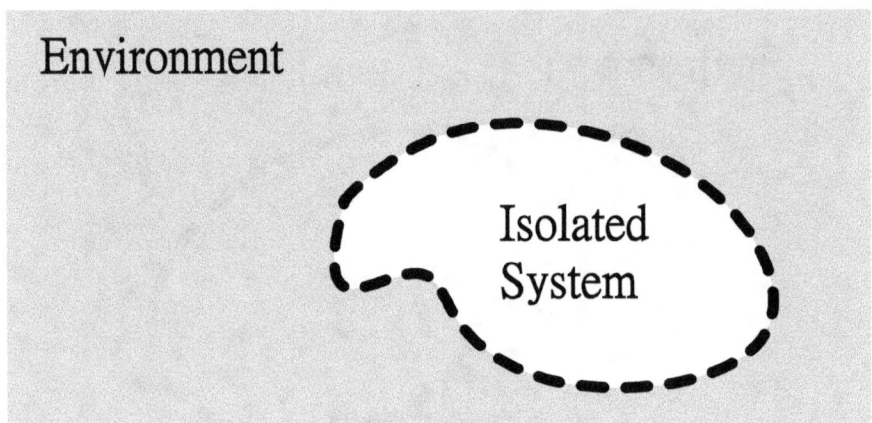

Figure 4-11 Isolated System does not Interrelate with the Environment

4-1-4 Evolution of a System

A system, not matter it is physical or conceptual, will always change from time to time. The change cause may come from the internal or external forces of the system. Cell division, as shown in Figure 4-12, is an example of the internal forces.

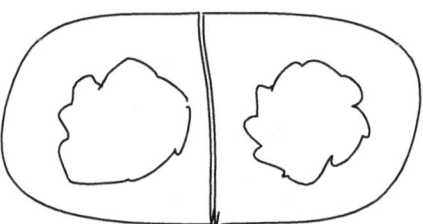

Figure 4-12 Cell Division

A worker reshaping, rebuilding, or remodeling a system, as shown in Figure 4-13, is an example of the external forces.

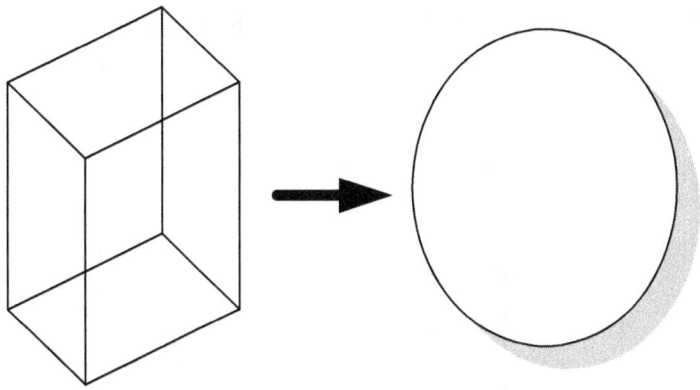

Figure 4-13   Reshapes a System

A system evolves when it changes. The evolution of a system is shown in Figure 4-14.

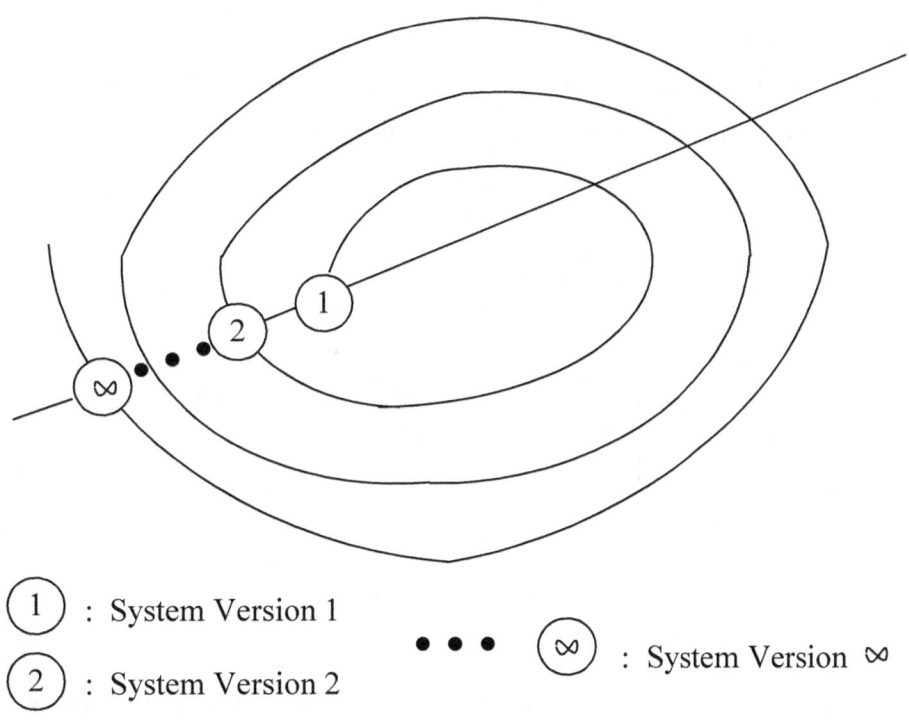

① : System Version 1

② : System Version 2

∞ : System Version ∞

Figure 4-14   Evolution of a System

Each time when a system changes or evolves, we shall get a new version of its definition. In the above figure, *version 1* stands for the original systems theory 1.0 definition and evolves into *version 2*, *version 3*,…, and *version* ∞ gradually.

For example, Figure 4-15 shows the *systems theory 1.0 version 1* defining the *house_B* hopefully to be an integrated whole, embodied in its assembled components of *roof_1*, *window_1* and *door_1*, their interrelationships with each other and the environment.

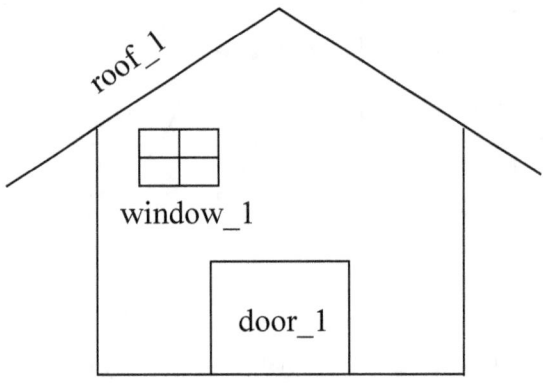

Figure 4-15   *Systems Theory 1.0 Version 1* Defining the *House_B*

After the *house_B* changes and evolves, Figure 4-16 shows the *systems theory 1.0 version 2* defining the *house_B* hopefully to be an integrated whole, embodied in its assembled components of *roof_1*, *window_1*, *window_2* and *door_1*, their interrelationships with each other and the environment.

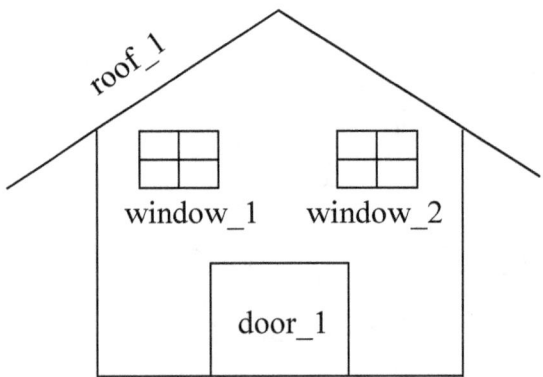

Figure 4-16   *Systems Theory 1.0 Version 2* Defining the *House_B*

4-1-5 High Order Systems

High order systems, also known as second order systems, interrelate with the environment through the exchange of not only matter, energy, data, information, or message but also versions of system, as shown in Figure 4-17.

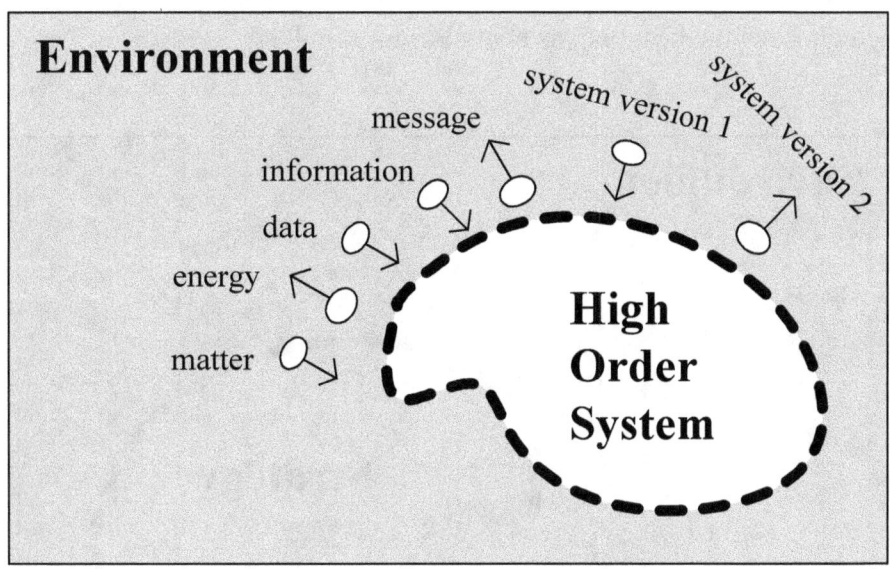

Figure 4-17   High Order Systems

System's learning, growing, change and evolution, are created by the human brain, strategy, or creative thinking. Human brain, strategy, creative thinking, system dynamics, etc. are regarded as a high order system. The human brain is a high order system, because it is able to produce a large number of systems versions, as shown in Figure 4-18.

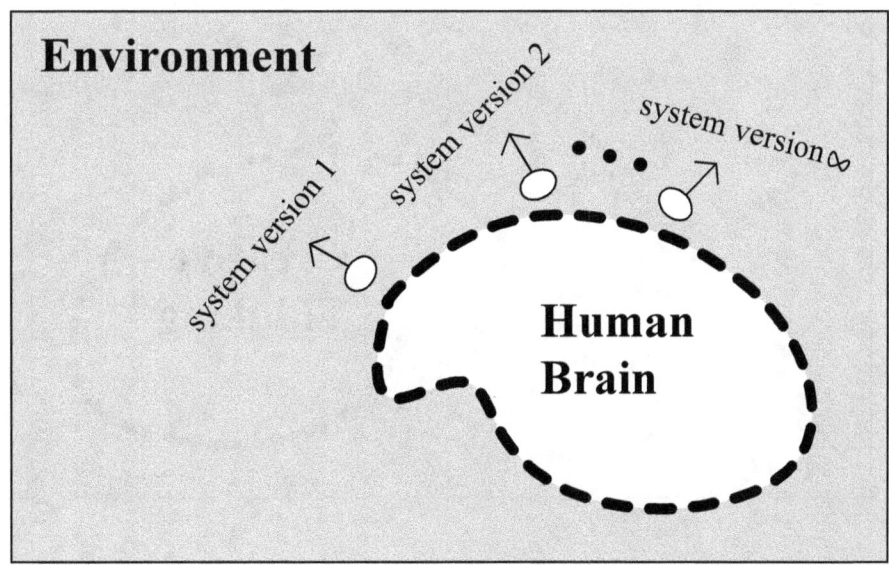

Figure 4-18   Human Brain is a High Order System

Strategy is a high order system because it creates a large number of systems versions then chooses the best one, as shown in Figure 4-19.

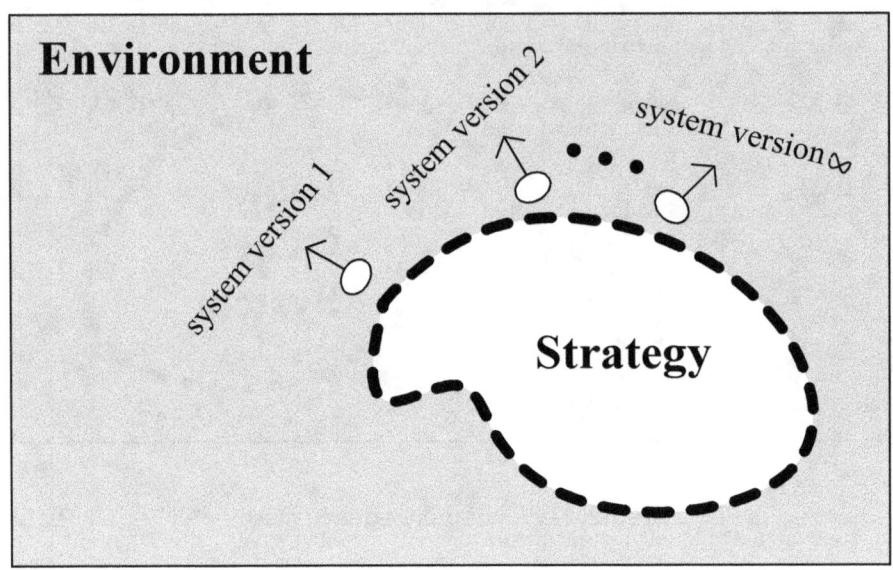

Figure 4-19   Strategy is a High Order System

Creative thinking is also a high order system, because it generates a large number of systems versions then chooses the best one, as shown in Figure 4-20.

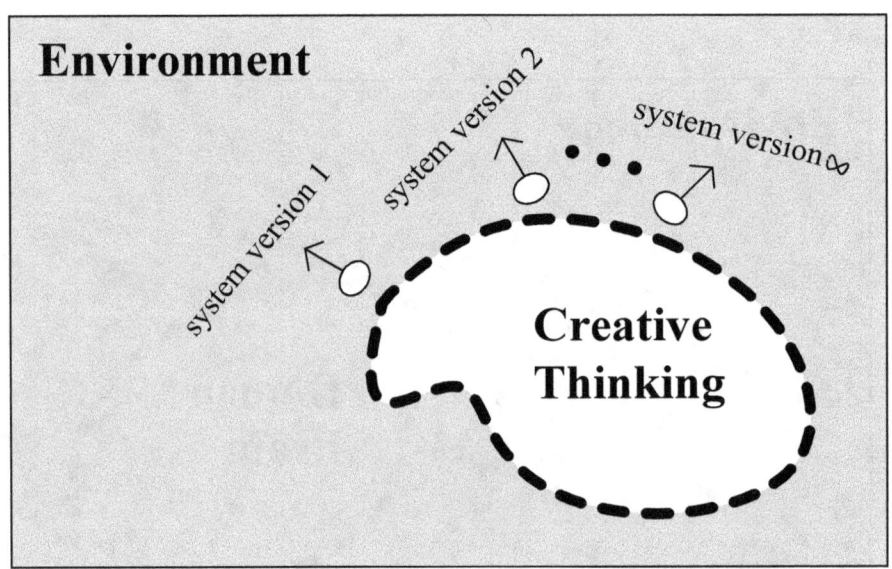

Figure 4-20   Creative Thinking is a High Order System

System dynamics is also a higher-order system, because it dynamically simulates the causal relationship among a large number of systems as shown in Figure 4-21. From these simulated systems, decision makers thus are able to strategically choose the most appropriate one.

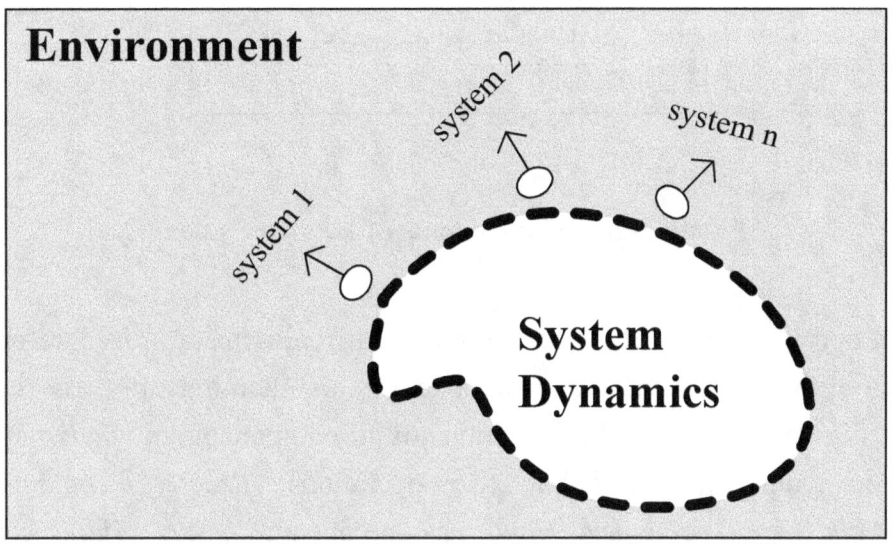

Figure 4-21   System Dynamics is a Higher-Order System

4-2 Systems Structure and Systems Behavior

Systems structure and systems behavior are the two most significant views of a system. Systems structure, defined by components, their operations and their composition, refers to the type of connection between the components of a system. Systems behavior, defined by the interrelationships between and among the environment and components, refers to the actions a system in conjunction with its environment.

4-2-1 Structure of Systems

Every system forms a whole. In general, structure of systems is the type of connection between the components of a system. More specifically, we define the structure of a system by 1) components, 2) their operations and 3) their composition.

Components are something relatively indivisible in one system. For example, *Head*, *Hands* and *Feet* are components of a *robot* system as shown in Figure 4-22.

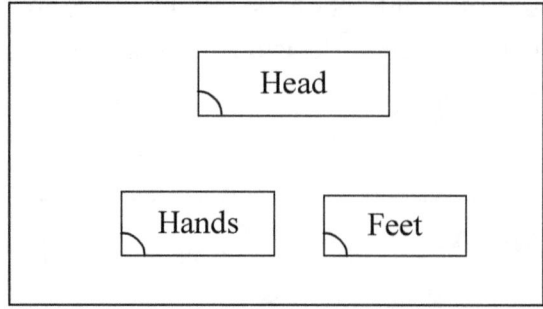

Figure 4-22   Components of a *Robot* System

An operation provided by each component represents a procedure or method or function of the component. Each component in a system must possess at least one operation. Figure 4-23 shows the operations of all components of a *robot* system. In the figure, component *Head* has two operations: *Receive_Write_Signal* and *Receive_Walk_Signal*; component *Hands* has one operation: *Move_Hand*; component *Feet* has one operation: *Move_Foot*.

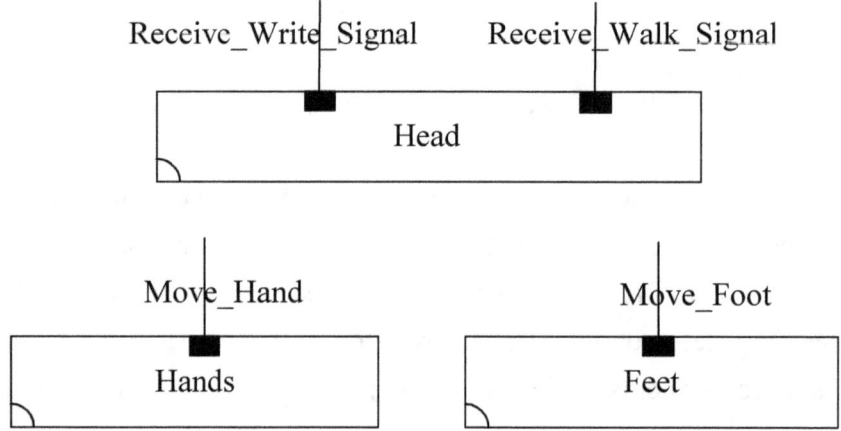

Figure 4-23   Operations of all Components of a *Robot* System

Composition of components defines the structural composition and decomposition of a system. For example, Figure 4-24 shows that in a *robot* system *Robot* is structurally composed of *Head* and *Limb*; *Limb* is structurally composed of *Hands* and *Feet*.

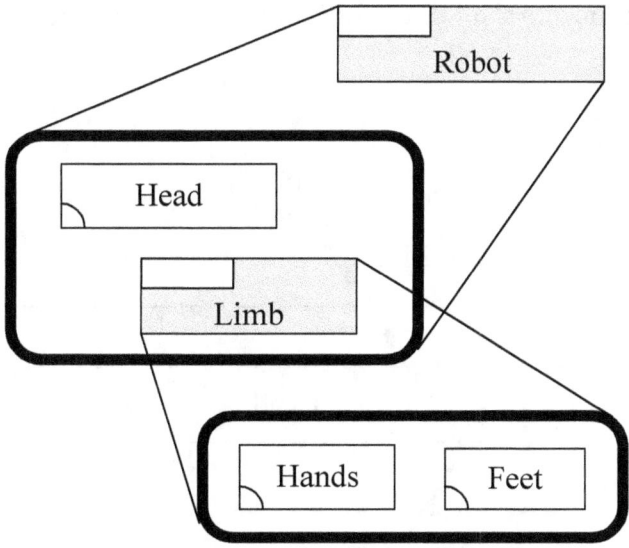

Figure 4-24   Composition of a *Robot* System

4-2-2 Behavior of Systems

Systems behavior refers to the interrelationships a system in conjunction with its environment. It is the response of the system to various stimuli, whether internal or external, conscious or subconscious, overt or covert, and voluntary or involuntary.

For example, Figure 4-25 demonstrates two individual behaviors: *Writing* and *Walking* that refers to the interrelationships a *robot* system in conjunction with its environment.

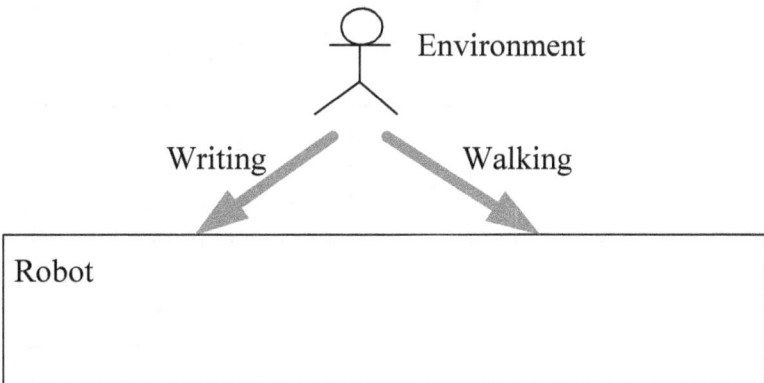

Figure 4-25   Behaviors of the *Robot* System

For each behavior, the environment always initiates the interrelationship and will lead more follow-up interrelationships to be executed among components. For example, Figure 4-26 demonstrates that interrelationships among the environment and the *Head*, *Hand*s components shall draw forth the *Writing* behavior.

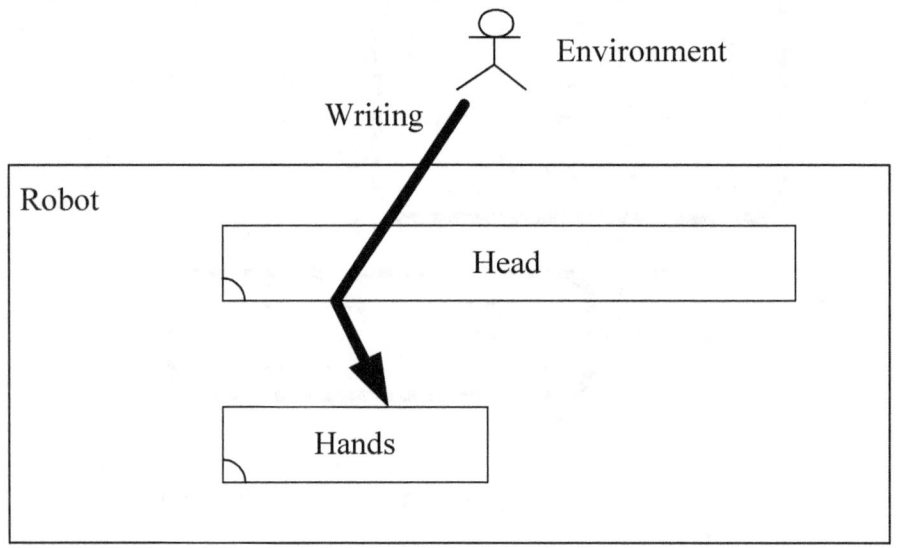

Figure 4-26   Interrelationships that Draw forth the *Writing* Behavior.

As a second example, Figure 4-27 demonstrates that interrelationships among the environment and the *Head*, *Feet* components shall draw forth the *Walking* behavior.

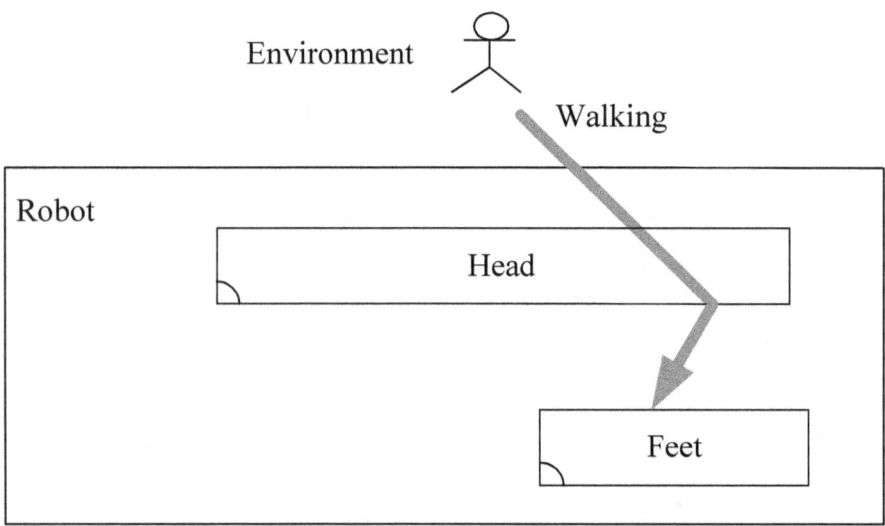

Figure 4-27   Interrelationships that Draw forth the Walking Behavior.

4-3 Structure-Behavior Coalescence

A system has been defined hopefully to be an integrated whole, embodied in its assembled components, their interrelationships with each other and the environment. Since systems structure and systems behavior are the two most prominent views of a system, integrating the systems structure and behavior apparently is the best way to achieve a truly integrated whole of a system. Since systems theory 1.0 does not describe the integration of systems structure and systems behavior, very likely it will never be able to actually form an integrated whole of a system.

Structure-behavior coalescence (SBC) demands the integration the structure and behavior, and hence achieves a truly integrated whole, of a system. A truly integrated whole sets a path for achieving the desired systems definition. SBC facilitates a truly integrated whole. Therefore, we conclude that SBC sets a path for achieving the systems definition. Systems theory 2.0 (Architectural theory) adopts the SBC approach and is highly adequate in defining a system.

4-3-1 Integrated Whole to Achieve the Systems Definition

A system has been defined hopefully to be an integrated whole, embodied in its assembled components, their interrelationships with each other and the environment. In other words, an integrated whole sets a path to achieve the systems definition as shown in Figure 4-28.

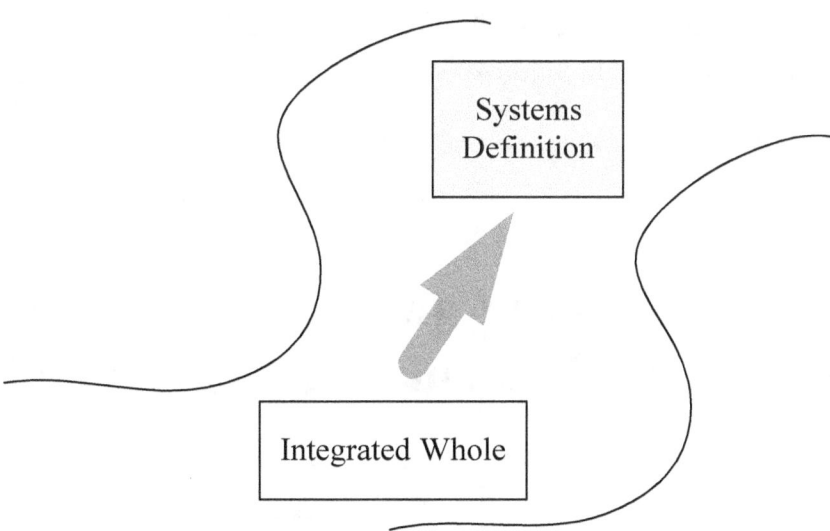

Figure 4-28   Integrated Whole to Achieve the Systems Definition

We conclude that in the systems definition, one integrated whole must be attached to or built on one systems structure. In other words, an integrated whole shall not exist alone; it must be loaded on a systems structure just like a cargo is loaded on a ship as shown in Figure 4-29. There will be no integrated whole if there is no systems structure. A stand-alone integrated whole with no systems structure is not meaningful.

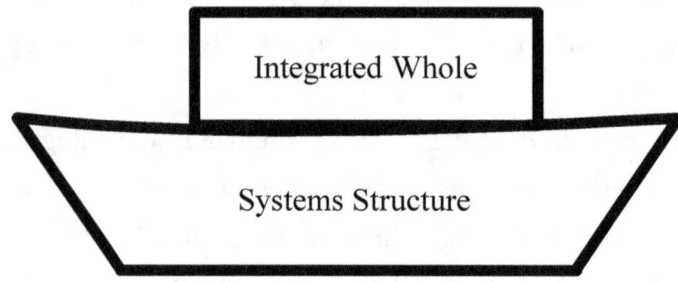

Figure 4-29   An Integrated Whole Must be Loaded on a Systems Structure

4-3-2 Integrating the Systems Structures and Systems Behaviors

By integrating the systems structures and systems behaviors, we obtain structure-behavior coalescence (SBC) within a system. Since systems structures and systems behaviors are so tightly integrated, we sometimes claim that the core theme of structure-behavior coalescence is: "Systems Architecture = Systems Structure + Systems Behavior," as shown in Figure 4-30.

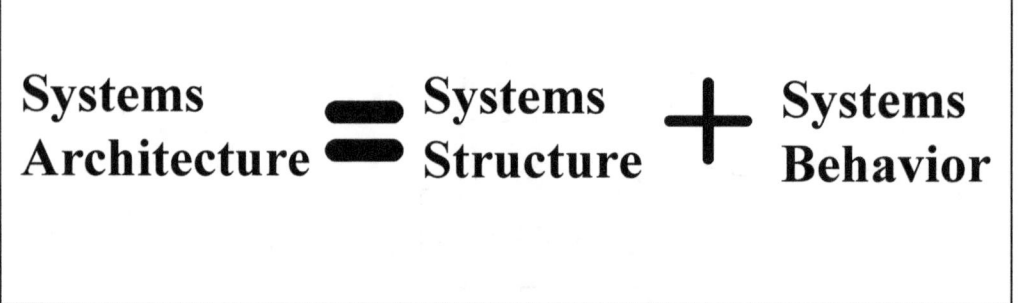

Figure 4-30   Core Theme of Structure-Behavior Coalescence

So far, integrating the systems structure and systems behavior has never been mentioned or proposed except the SBC architecture and object-process methodology (OPM). In most cases, systems behaviors are separated from systems structures when defining a system.

4-3-3 Structure-Behavior Coalescence to Facilitate an Integrated Whole

Since systems structure and systems behavior are the two most prominent characteristics of a system, integrating the systems structure and systems behavior apparently is the best way to achieve a truly integrated whole of a system. If we are not able to integrate the systems structure and systems behavior, then there is no way that we are able to integrate the whole system. In other words, structure-behavior coalescence facilitates an integrated whole as shown in Figure 4-31.

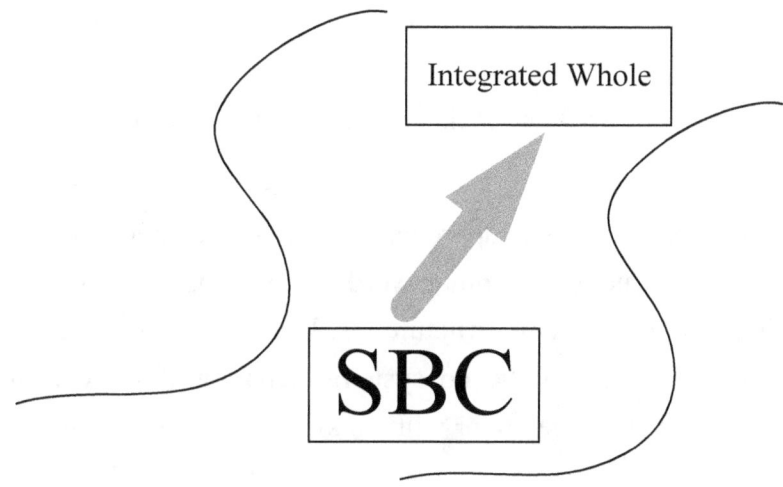

Figure 4-31   SBC Facilitates an Integrated Whole

Since systems theory 1.0 does not describe the integration of systems structure and systems behavior, very likely it only hopes and will never be able to form an integrated whole of a system. In this situation, systems theory 1.0 is incompetent in defining a system appropriately.

4-3-4 Structure-Behavior Coalescence to Achieve the Systems Definition

Figure 4-29 declares that an integrated whole sets a path to achieve the desired systems definition. Figure 4-32 declares that structure-behavior coalescence facilitates an integrated whole.

Combining the above two declarations, we conclude that the structure-behavior coalescence (SBC) method sets a path to achieve the systems definition as shown in Figure 4-32.

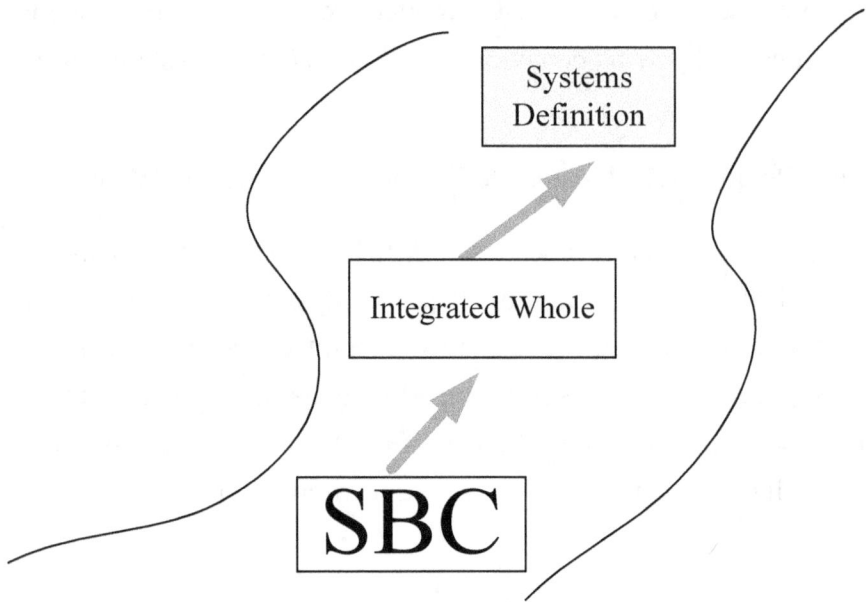

Figure 4-32   SBC to Achieve the Systems Definition

We conclude that in the SBC approach, a systems behavior must be attached to or built on a systems structure. In other words, a systems behavior can not exist alone; it must be loaded on a systems structure just like a cargo is loaded on a ship as shown in Figure 4-33. There will be no systems behavior if there is no systems structure. A stand-alone systems behavior with no systems structure is not meaningful.

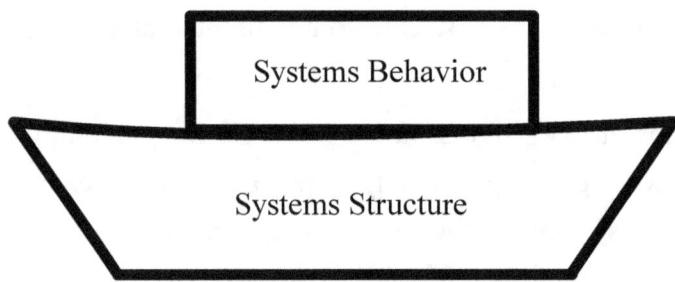

Figure 4-33   A Systems Behavior Must be Loaded on a Systems Structure

4-3-5 Systems Theory 2.0 Defining a System

Since structure-behavior coalescence grows into an important ingredient in defining a system, we shall include it in the definition of a system. Figure 4-34 shows that how the systems theory 2.0 (architectural theory) defining a system.

> A system,
> through structure-behavior coalescence (SBC),
> truly is an integrated whole,
> embodied in its assembled components, their interactions with each other and the environment.

Figure 4-34　Systems Theory 2.0 Defining a System

Using the systems theory 2.0 (architectural theory) defining a system has the following characteristics: 1) it emphasizes the system's structure-behavior coalescence; 2) it is a truly integrated whole; 3) it is embodied in its assembled components; and 4) components are interacting (or handshaking) with each other and the environment.

Structure-behavior coalescence (SBC) provides a sophisticated way to integrate the structure and behavior of a system. Systems theory 2.0 (Architectural theory) adopts the SBC architecture description language (SBC-ADL) to formally define the essence of a system and its details at the same time. SBC-ADL contains six fundamental diagrams: a) architecture hierarchy diagram, b) framework diagram, c) component operation diagram, d) component connection diagram, e) structure-behavior coalescence diagram and f) interaction flow diagram.

So far, we have introduced the systems theory 2.0 (architectural theory) defining a system. In the following chapters, we shall delineate the details of SBC-ADL.

PART II: SBC ARCHITECTURE DESCRIPTION LANGUAGE

50

Chapter 5: Architecture Hierarchy Diagram

Systems theory 2.0 (Architectural theory) uses an architecture hierarchy diagram (AHD) to define the multi-level decomposition and composition of a system. AHD is the first fundamental diagram to achieve structure-behavior coalescence.

5-1 Decomposition and Composition

The following is an example of systems decomposition and composition. The *Computer* system consists of *Monitor, Keyboard, Mouse* and *Case*, as shown in Figure 5-1. The *Monitor, Keyboard, Mouse* and *Case* are subsystems that comprise the *Computer* system.

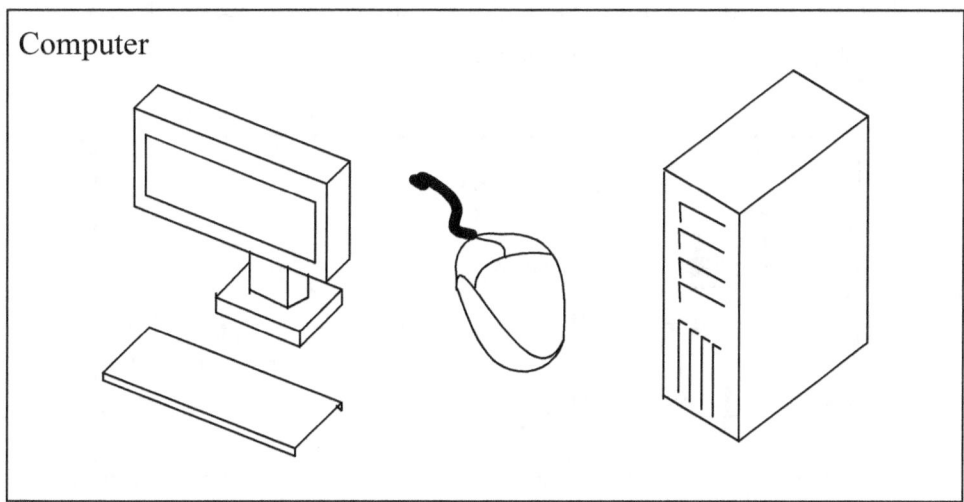

Figure 5-1   Decomposition and Composition of the *Computer* System

Another example indicates that the *Tree* system is composed of *Root* and *Stem*, as shown in Figure 5-2. In this example, we would say that the *Root* and *Stem* are subsystems, respectively, while the *Tree* system consists of its subsystems.

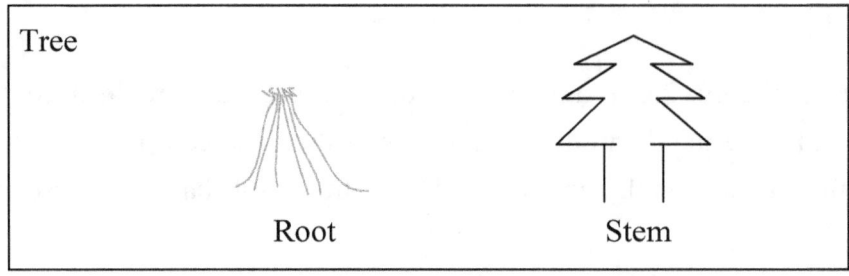

Figure 5-2   Decomposition and Composition of the *Tree* System

The last example demonstrates that the *SBC_Book* system is composed of *Chapter_1*, *Part_1* and *Part_2*, as shown in Figure 5-3. In this example, we would say that the *Chapter_1*, *Part_1* and *Part_2* are subsystems, respectively while the *SBC_Book* system consists of its subsystems.

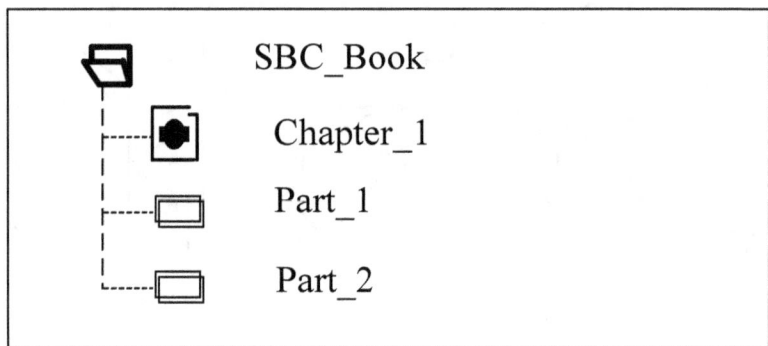

Figure 5-3   Decomposition and Composition of the *SBC_Book* System

The architecture hierarchy diagram (AHD) is used to define the decomposition and composition of a system. As an example, the AHD of the *Computer* system is shown in Figure 5-4. We clearly observe that *Computer* is composed of *Monitor*, *Keyboard*, *Mouse* and *Case*.

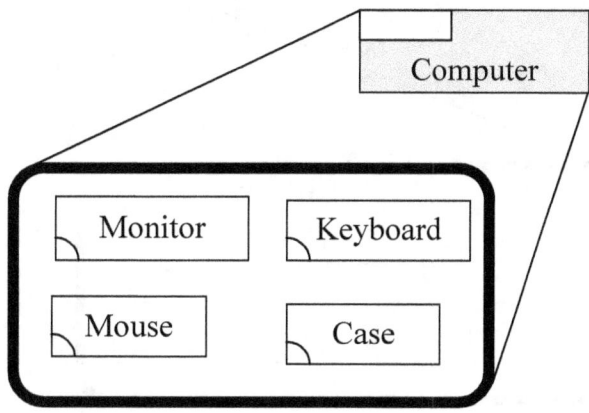

Figure 5-4   AHD of the *Computer* System

As a second example, Figure 5-5 shows the AHD of the *Tree* system. We clearly observe that *Tree* is composed of *Root* and *Stem*.

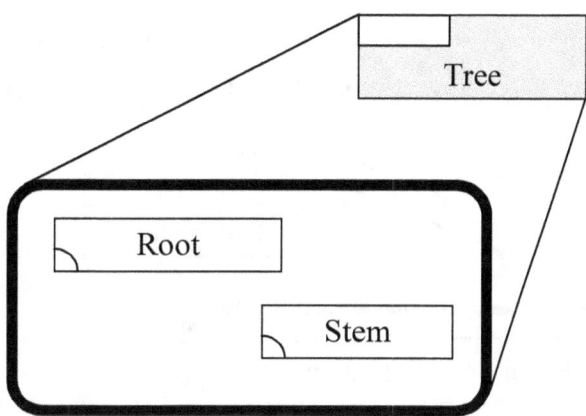

Figure 5-5   AHD of *Tree* System

As a third example, Figure 5-6 shows the AHD of the *SBC_Book* system. We clearly observe that *SBC_Book* is composed of *Chapter_1*, *Part_1* and *Part_2*.

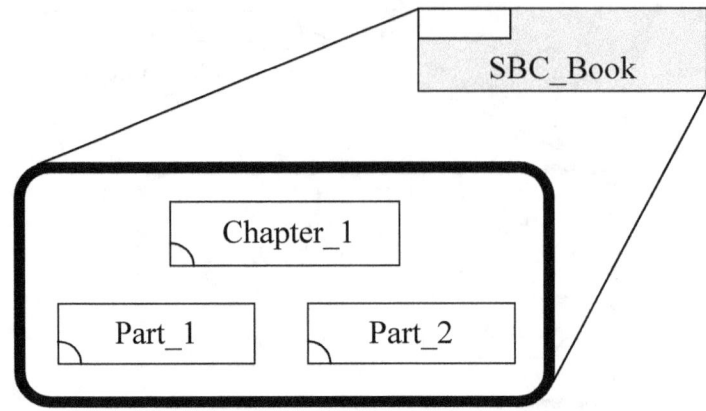

Figure 5-6   AHD of the *SBC_Book* system

5-2 Multi-Level Decomposition and Composition

The subsystem may also contain subsystems as we further decompose it. For example, *Case* is a subsystem of *Computer*, and we further decompose it into *Motherboard*, *Hard_Disk*, *Power_Supply* and *DVD_Disk*, as shown in Figure 5-7.

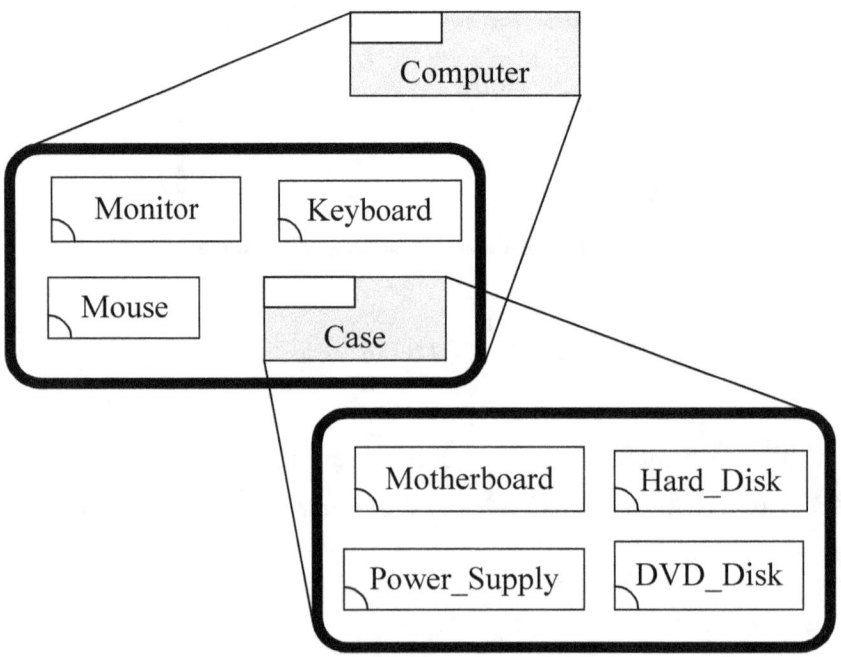

Figure 5-7 Multi-Level Decomposition/Composition of the *Computer* System

As a second example, *Stem* is a subsystem of *Tree*, and we further decompose it into *Trunk* and *Leaf*, as shown in Figure 5-8.

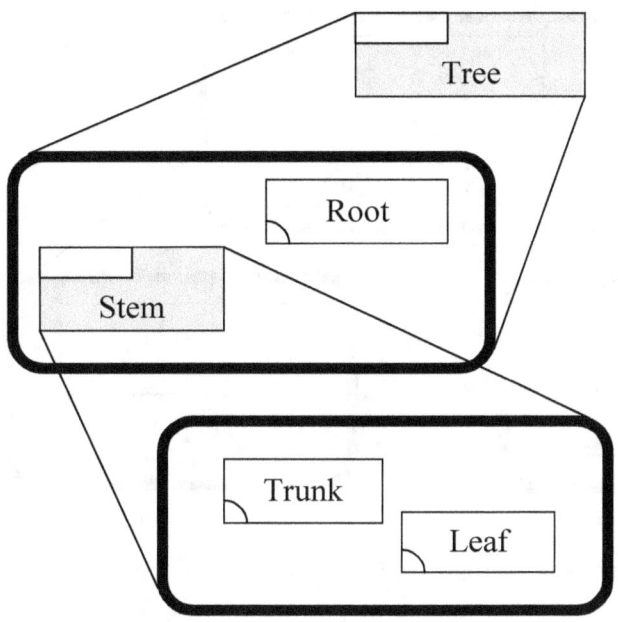

Figure 5-8 Multi-Level Decomposition/Composition of the *Tree* System

As a third example, *Part_1* is a subsystem of *SBC_Book*, and we further decompose it into *Chapter_2* and *Chapter_3*; *Part_2* is also a subsystem of *SBC_Book*, and we further decompose it into *Chapter_4* and *Chapter_5*, as shown in Figure 5-9.

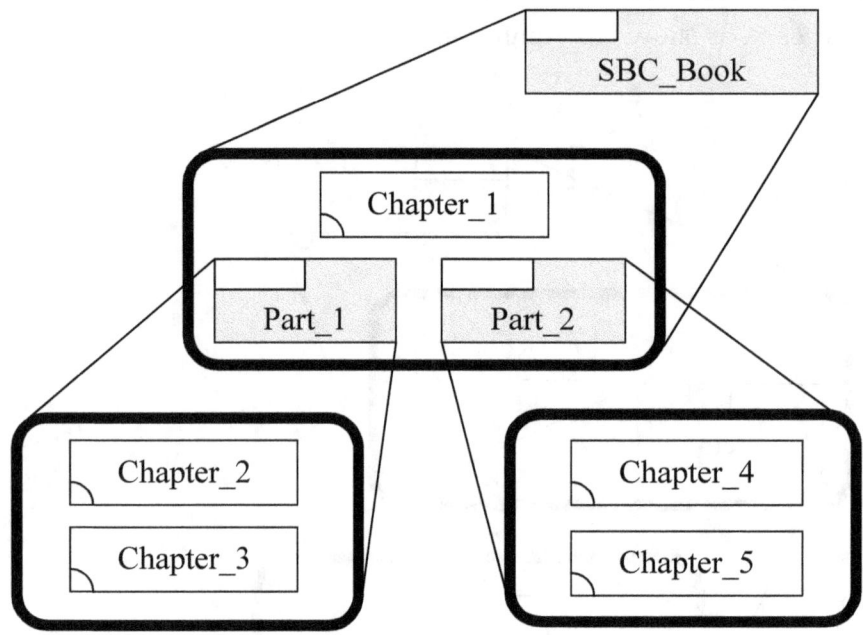

Figure 5-9   Multi-Level Decomposition/Composition of the *SBC_Book* System

Generally speaking, multi-level decomposition and composition of a system is applied often in defining a system. To make a complex system look simple, the mechanism of multi-level composition and decomposition should be utilized.

5-3 Aggregated and Non-Aggregated Systems

Any system (at any level) involved with multi-level decomposition and composition of a system is either aggregated or non-aggregated. The definition of aggregated and non-aggregated systems is shown in Figure 5-10.

> Definition of Aggregated Systems:
>
> A system (within an AHD) is aggregated if it is composed of any sub-system.
>
> ---
>
> Definition of Non-aggregated Systems
>
> A system (within an AHD) is non-aggregated if it is NOT composed of any sub-system.

Figure 5-10   Definition of Aggregated and Non-aggregated Systems

Non-aggregated systems are sometimes referred to as components, parts, entities and objects.

In the multi-level systems decomposition and composition, any system is either aggregated or non-aggregated, but not both. For example, in Figure 5-4, *Case* is a non-aggregated system, not an aggregated system. As an interesting contrast, in Figure 5-7, *Case* is an aggregated system, not a non-aggregated system.

As a second example, in Figure 5-5, *Stem* is a non-aggregated system, not an aggregated system. As an interesting contrast, in Figure 5-8, *Stem* is an aggregated system, not a non-aggregated system.

As a third example, in Figure 5-6, *Part_1* and *Part_2* are non-aggregated systems, not aggregated systems. As an interesting contrast, in Figure 5-9, *Part_1* and *Part_2* are aggregated systems, not non-aggregated systems.

Chapter 6: Framework Diagram

Systems theory 2.0 (Architectural theory) uses a framework diagram (FD) to define the multi-layer (also referred to as multi-tier) decomposition and composition of a system. FD is the second fundamental diagram to achieve structure-behavior coalescence.

6-1 Multi-Layer Decomposition and Composition

Decomposition and composition of a system can also be defined in a multi-layer manner. We draw a framework diagram (FD) for the multi-layer decomposition and composition of a system.

As an example, Figure 6-1 shows a FD of the *Computer* system. In the figure, *Technology_SubLayer_2* contains *Monitor*, *Keyboard* and *Mouse*; *Technology_SubLayer_1* contains *Motherboard*, *Hard_Disk*, *Power_Supply* and *DVD_Disk*.

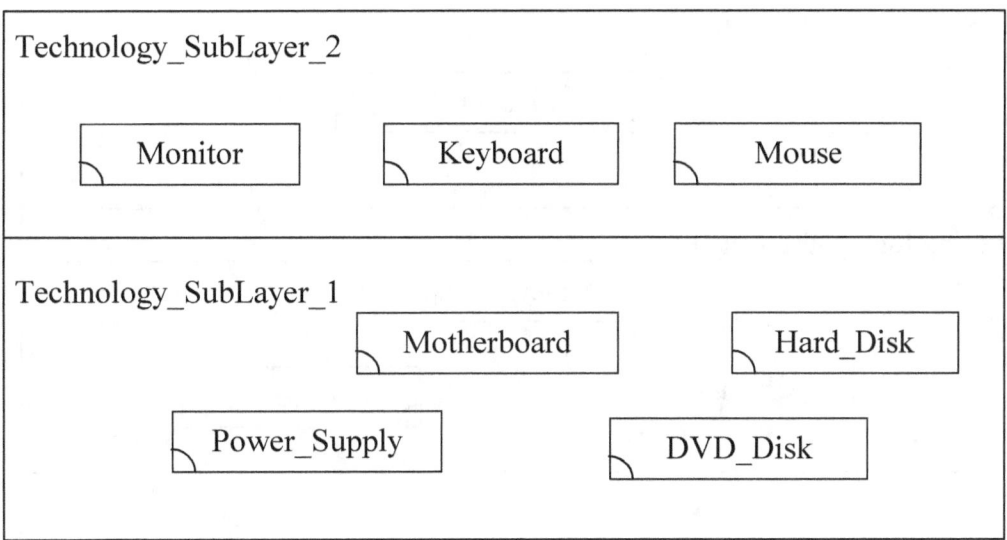

Figure 6-1　FD of the *Computer* System

As a second example, Figure 6-2 shows a FD of the *Tree* system. In the figure, *Technology_SubLayer_2* contains *Root*; *Technology_SubLayer_1* contains *Trunk* and *Leaf*.

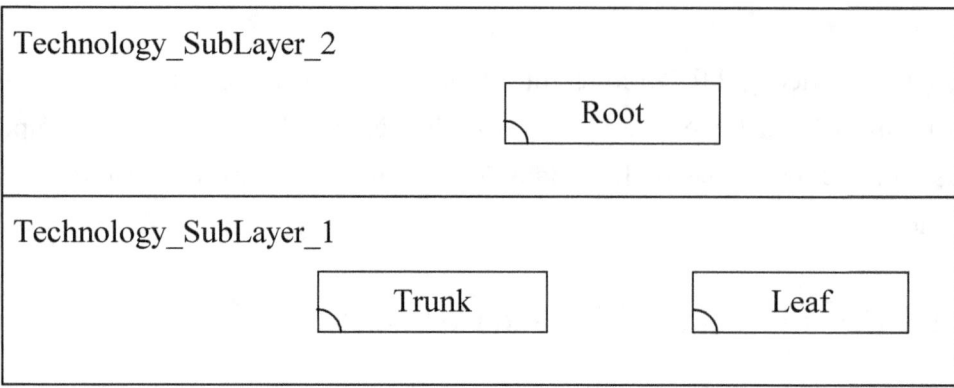

Figure 6-2   FD of the *Tree* System

As a third example, Figure 6-3 shows a FD of the *SBC_Book* system. In the figure, *Technology_SubLayer_2* contains *Chapter_1*; *Technology_SubLayer_1* contains *Chapter_2*, *Chapter_3*, *Chapter_4* and *Chapter_5*.

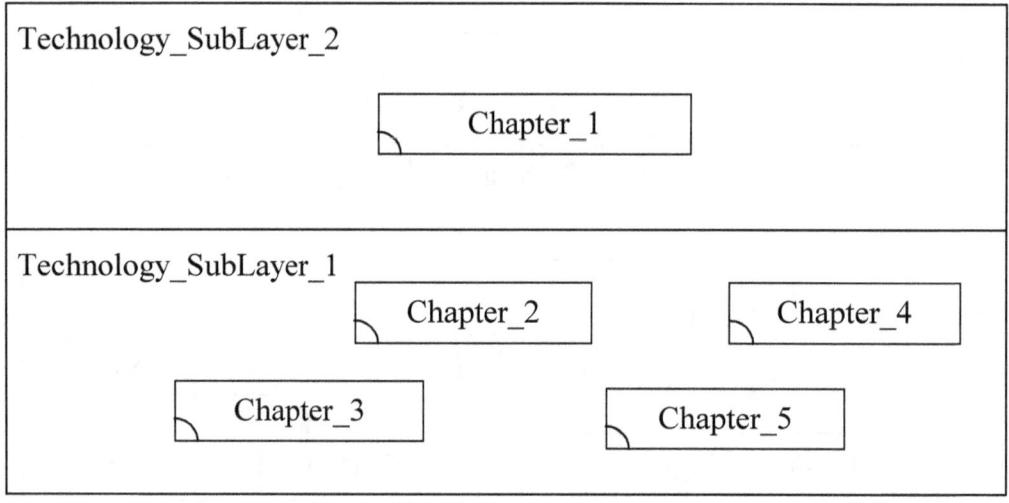

Figure 6-3   FD of the *SBC_Book* System

6-2 Only Non-Aggregated Systems Appear in Framework Diagrams

Both aggregated and non-aggregated systems are displayed in the multi-level AHD decomposition and composition of a system. As an interesting contrast, only non-aggregated systems shall appear in the multi-layer FD decomposition and composition of a system.

For example, Figure 5-7 in the previous chapter shows an AHD of the *Computer* system in which both aggregated systems such as *Computer*, *Case* and non-aggregated systems such as *Monitor*, *Keyboard*, *Mouse*, *Motherboard*, *Hard_Disk*, *Power_Supply*, *DVD_Disk* are displayed. As an interesting contrast, Figure 6-1 in the previous section shows a FD of the *Computer* system in which only non-aggregated systems such as *Monitor*, *Keyboard*, *Mouse*, *Motherboard*, *Hard_Disk*, *Power_Supply* and *DVD_Disk* are displayed.

For a second example, Figure 5-8 in the previous chapter shows an AHD of the *Tree* system in which both aggregated systems such as *Tree*, *Stem* and non-aggregated systems such as *Root*, *Trunk*, *Leaf* are displayed. As an interesting contrast, Figure 6-2 in the previous section shows a FD of the *Tree* system in which only non-aggregated systems such as *Root*, *Trunk* and *Leaf* are displayed.

For a third example, Figure 5-9 in the previous chapter shows an AHD of the *SBC_Book* system in which both aggregated systems such as *SBC_Book*, *Part_1*, *Part_2* and non-aggregated systems such as *Chapter_1*, *Chapter_2*, *Chapter_3*, *Chapter_4*, *Chapter_5* are displayed. As an interesting contrast, Figure 6-3 in the previous section shows a FD of the *SBC_Book* system in which only non-aggregated systems such as *Chapter_1*, *Chapter_2*, *Chapter_3*, *Chapter_4* and *Chapter_5* are displayed.

Chapter 7: Component Operation Diagram

Systems theory 2.0 (Architectural theory) uses a component operation diagram (COD) to define all components' operations of a system. COD is the third fundamental diagram to achieve structure-behavior coalescence.

7-1 Operations of Each Component

An operation provided by each component represents a procedure or method or function of the component. If other components request this component to perform an operation, then shall use it to accomplish the operation request.

Each component in a system must possess at least one operation. A component should not exist in a system if it does not possess any operation. Figure 7-1 shows that component *SalePurchase_GUI* has four operations: *SaleInputClick*, *SalePrintClick*, *PurchaseInputClick* and *PurchasePrintClick*.

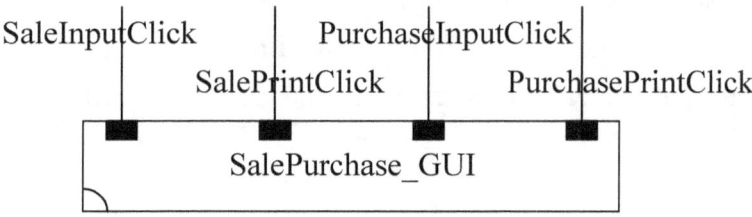

Figure 7-1   Four Operations of *SalePurchase_GUI*

An operation formula is utilized to fully define an operation. An operation formula includes a) operation name, b) input parameters and c) output parameters as shown in Figure 7-2.

Operation_Name (In $a_1, a_2, ..., a_M$; Out $a_{M+1}, a_{M+2}, ..., a_{M+N}$)

Figure 7-2   Operation Formula

Operation name is the name of this operation. In a system, every operation name should be unique. Duplicate operation names shall not be allowed in any system.

An operation may have several input and output parameters. The input and output parameters, gathered from all operations, represent the input data and output data views of a system. As shown in Figure 7-3, component *SalePrint_GUI* possesses the operation *ShowModal* which has no input/output parameter; component *SalePrint_GUI* also possesses the operation *SalePrintButtonClick* which has two input parameters *sDate* and *sNo* (with the arrow direction pointing to the component) and one output parameter *s_report* (with the arrow direction opposite to the component).

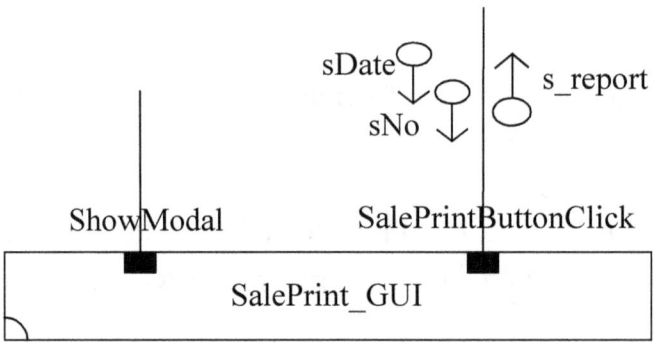

Figure 7-3   Input/Output Parameters of *SalePrintButtonClick*

Data formats of input and output parameters are defined by data type specifications. There are two groups of data types: primitive and composite. Figure 7-4 shows the primitive data type specification of the *sDate* and *sNo* input parameters occurring in the *SalePrintButtonClick(In sDate, sNo; Out s_report)* operation formula.

Parameter	Data Type	Instances
sDate	Text	20100517, 20100612
sNo	Text	881, 992

Figure 7-4　　Primitive Data Type Specifications

Figure 7-5 shows the composite data type specification of the *s_report* output parameter occurring in the *SalePrintButtonClick(In sDate, sNo; Out s_report)* operation formula.

Parameter	*s_report*
Data Type	TABLE of 　　Sale Date : Text 　　Sale No : Text 　　Customer : Text 　　ProductNo : Text 　　Quantity : Integer 　　UnitPrice : Real 　　Total : Real End TABLE;
Instances	Sale Date : 20100517　　Sale No : 001 Customer : Larry Fink | ProductNo | Quantity | UnitPrice | |---|---|---| | A12345 | 400 | 100.00 | | A00001 | 300 | 200.00 | 　　　　　　　　　　　　Total : 100,000.00

Figure 7-5　　Composite Data Type Specifications

7-2 Drawing the Component Operation Diagram

We use a component operation diagram (COD to define all components' operations of a system. Figure 7-6 shows a COD of the *Multi-Tier Personal Data System*. In the figure, component *MTPDS_GUI* has two operations: *Calculate_AgeClick* and *Calculate_OverweightClick*; component *Age_Logic* has one operation: *Calculate_Age*; component *Overweight_Logic* has one operation: *Calculate_Overweight*; component *Personal_Database* has two operations: *Sql_DateOfBirth_Select* and *Sql_SexHeightWeight_Select*.

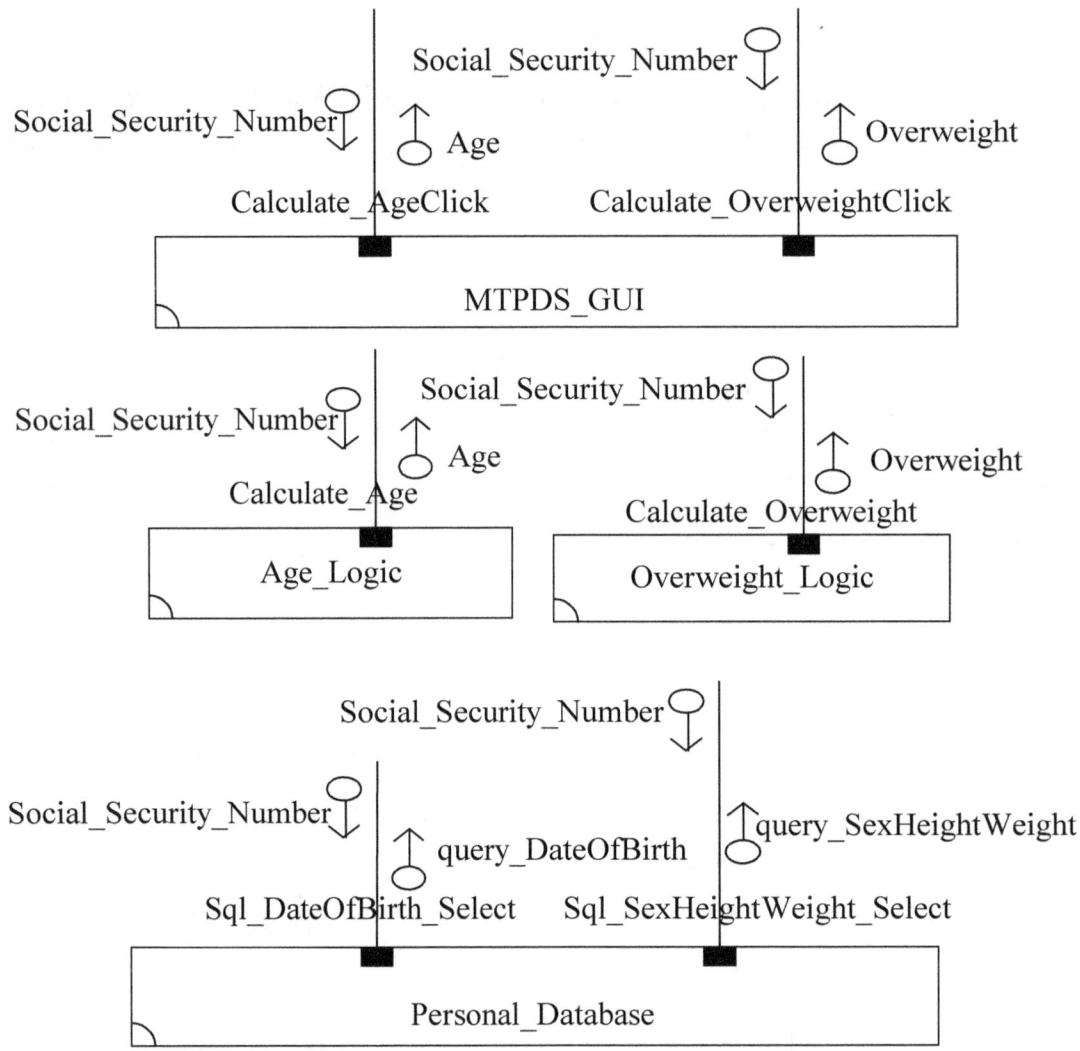

Figure 7-6   COD of the *Multi-Tier Personal Data System*

The operation formula of *Calculate_AgeClick* is *Calculate_AgeClick(In Social_Security_Number; Out Age)*. The operation formula of *Calculate_OverweightClick* is *Calculate_OverweightClick(In*

Social_Security_Number; Out Overweight). The operation formula of *Calculate_Age* is *Calculate_Age(In Social_Security_Number; Out Age)*. The operation formula of *Calculate_Overweight* is *Calculate_Overweight(In Social_Security_Number; Out Overweight)*. The operation formula of *Sql_DateOfBirth_Select* is *Sql_DateOfBirth_Select(In Social_Security_Number; Out query_DateOfBirth)*. The operation formula of *Sql_SexHeightWeight_Select* is *Sql_SexHeightWeight_Select(In Social_Security_Number; Out query_SexHeightWeight)*.

Figure 7-7 shows the primitive data type specification of the *Social_Security_Number* input parameter and the *Age, Overweight* output parameters.

Parameter	Data Type	Instances
Social_Security_Number	Text	424-87-3651, 512-24-3722
Age	Integer	28, 56
Overweight	Boolean	Yes, No

Figure 7-7   Primitive Data Type Specification

Figure 7-8 shows the composite data type specification of the *query_DateOfBirth* output parameter occurring in the *Sql_DateOfBirth_Select(In Social_Security_Number; Out query_DateOfBirth)* operation formula.

Parameter	*query_DateOfBirth*

Data Type	TABLE of
	   Social_Security_Number : Text
	   Age : Integer
	End TABLE ;

Instances	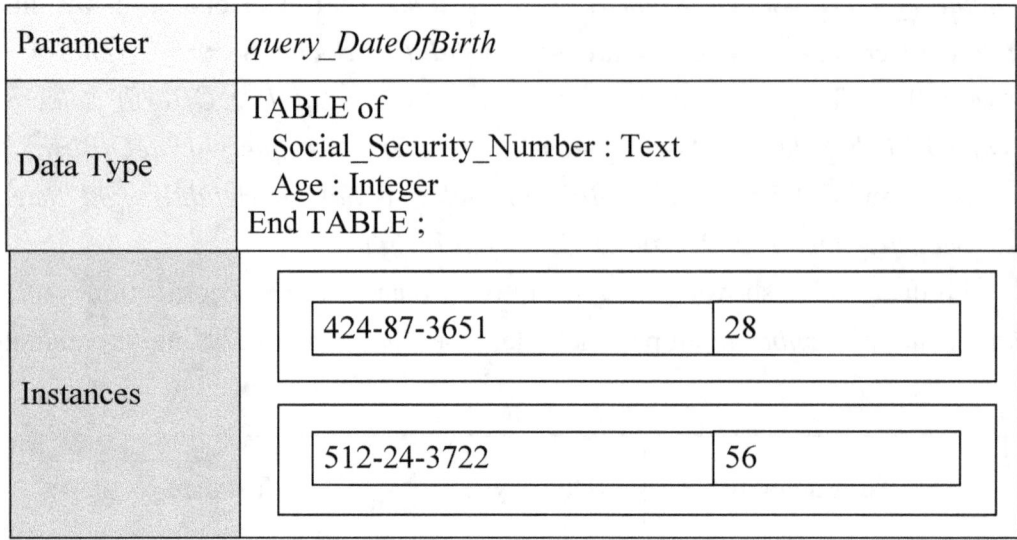

Figure 7-8   Composite Data Type Specifications

Figure 7-9 shows the composite data type specification of the *query_SexHeightWeight* output parameter occurring in the *Sql_SexHeightWeight_Select(In Social_Security_Number; Out query_SexHeightWeight)* operation formula.

Parameter	*query_SexHeightWeight*

Data Type	TABLE of
	   Social_Security_Number : Text
	   Sex : Text
	   Height : Number
	   Weight : Number
	End TABLE ;

Instances	424-87-3651 Female 162 76 512-24-3722 Male 180 80

Figure 7-9   Composite Data Type Specifications

Chapter 8: Component Connection Diagram

Systems theory 2.0 (Architectural theory) uses a component connection diagram (CCD) to define how all components and actors are connected within a system. CCD is the fourth fundamental diagram to achieve structure-behavior coalescence.

8-1 Essence of a Connection

A connection implies an operation request. When an operation is used by another subsystem then a connection appears. Accordingly, a connection is defined as the linkage that is constructed when an operation is used by another subsystem. Figure 8-1 shows that Sub*system_A* uses the *Salary_Calculation* operation provided by the *Component_B* component.

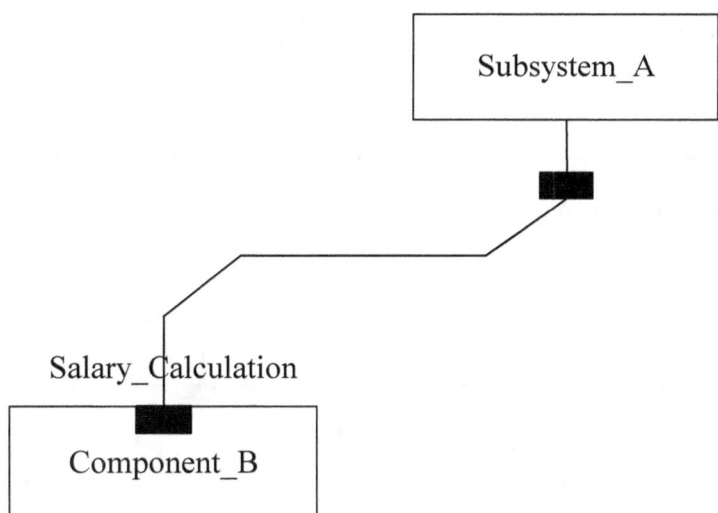

Figure 8-1   A Connection Appears When an Operation is Used

The above figure describes, sufficiently, the essence of a connection. However, we seldom use this kind of drawing. Instead, a simplified drawing of the above figure is often used as shown in Figure 8-2.

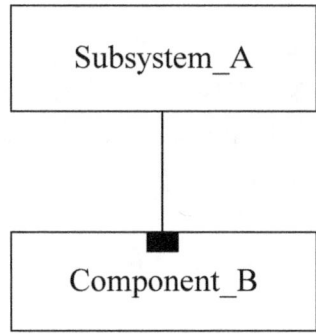

Figure 8-2   Simplified Drawing of a Connection

Since an operation is always provided by a component, there is no doubt that the *Component_B* operation provider is a component. On the contrary, the *Subsystem_A* operation user can be either a component (e.g., *Component_A*) or an actor (e.g., *Actor_A*) as shown in Figure 8-3. An actor belongs to the external environment of a system.

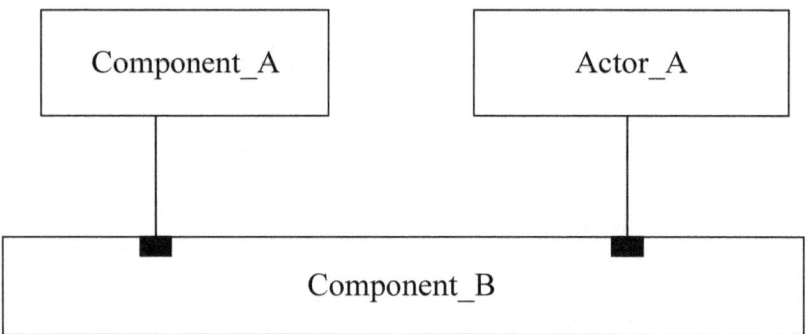

Figure 8-3   Operation User is either a Component or an Actor

Within a connection the subsystem (either a component or an actor) using the operation is always entitled the *Client* and the component which provides the operation is always entitled the *Server* as Figure 8-4 shows.

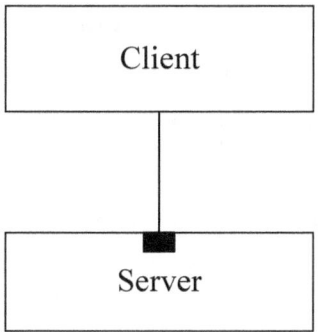

Figure 8-4   Roles of Client and Server Within a Connection

8-2 Drawing the Component Connection Diagrams

A component connection diagram (CCD) is utilized to define how all components and actors (in the external environment) are connected within a system. Figure 8-5 exhibits the *Multi-Tier Personal Data System's COD*.

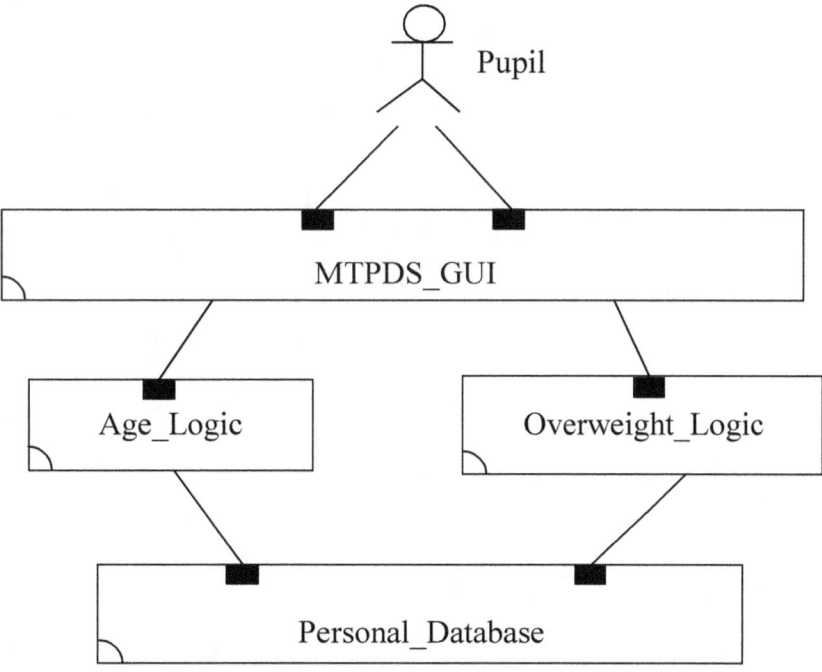

Figure 8-5   CCD of the *Multi-Tier Personal Data System*

In Figure 8-5, actor *Pupil* has two connections with the *MTPDS_GUI* component; component *MTPDS_GUI* has one connection with each of the *Age_Logic* and *Overweight_Logic* components; component *Age_Logic* has a connection with the *Personal_Database* component; component *Overweight_Logic* has a connection with the *Personal_Database* component.

After finishing the CCD, the formation pattern of the *Multi-Tier Personal Data System* will be constructed; thus the systems structure of the *Multi-Tier Personal Data System* becomes more transparent.

Chapter 9: Structure-Behavior Coalescence Diagram

Systems theory 2.0 (Architectural theory) uses a structure-behavior coalescence diagram (SBCD) to define the systems structure and systems behavior coexisting in a system. SBCD is the fifth fundamental diagram to achieve structure-behavior coalescence.

9-1 Purpose of Structure-Behavior Coalescence Diagram

The major aim of SBC architecture description language is to achieve the integration of systems structure and systems behavior within a system. SBCD enables us to observe the systems structure and systems behavior coexisting in a system. This is the purpose of utilizing SBCD when defining a system.

Figure 9-1 exhibits a SBCD of the *Multi-Tier Personal Data System*. In this example, interactions among the *Pupil* actor and the *MTPDS_GUI*, *Age_Logic*, *Overweight_Logic*, *Personal_Database* components shall draw forth the *AgeCalculation* and *OverweightCalculation* behaviors.

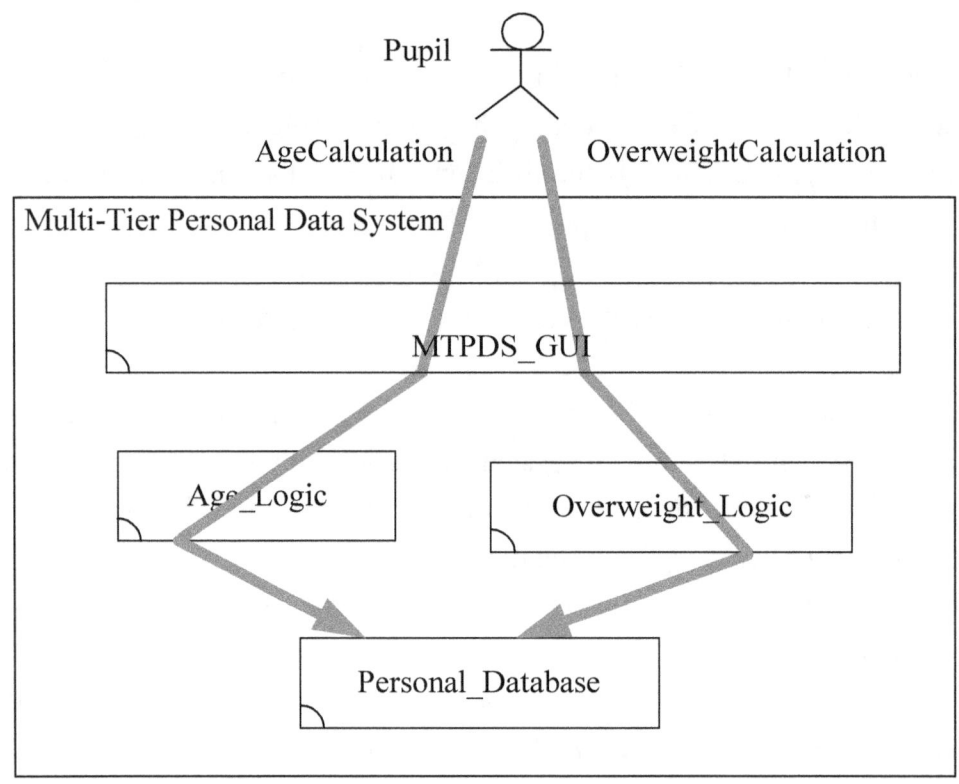

Figure 9-1   SBCD of the *Multi-Tier Personal Data System*

The overall behavior of a system is the aggregation of all its individual behaviors. All individual behaviors are mutually independent of each other. They tend to be executed in parallel [Hoar85, Miln89, Miln99]. For example, the overall behavior of the *Multi-Tier Personal Data System* includes the *AgeCalculation* and *OverweightCalculation* behaviors. In other words, the *AgeCalculation* and *OverweightCalculation* behaviors are combined to produce the overall behavior of the *Multi-Tier Personal Data System*.

The major purpose of using SBC architecture description language is to achieve the integration of systems structure and systems behavior within a system. In Figure 9-1, we are able to define the systems structure and systems behavior coexisting in a SBCD. That is, in the *Multi-Tier Personal Data System*'s SBCD, we not only see its systems structure but also see (at the same time) its systems behavior.

9-2 Drawing the Structure-Behavior Coalescence Diagrams

Let us now explain the usage of SBCD by constructing a SBCD step by step.

The goal of having a SBCD is enabling us to see both the systems structure and systems behavior, simultaneously. In order to achieve this goal, a SBCD is drawn by first defining all of the components, then defining the external environment's actors, and finally defining the interactions among these components and the external environment's actors.

For example, the *Multi-Tier Personal Data System* has two behaviors: *AgeCalculation* and *OverweightCalculation*. After constructing the *Multi-Tier Personal Data System* with all its components, the external environment's actors and the *AgeCalculation* behavior, we obtain the graphical representation as shown in Figure 9-2. In this Figure, the *AgeCalculation* behavior indicates that actor *Pupil* interacts with the *MTPDS_GUI* component first, then component *MTPDS_GUI* interacts with the *Age_Logic* component later, then component *Age_Logic* interacts with the *Personal_Database* component finally.

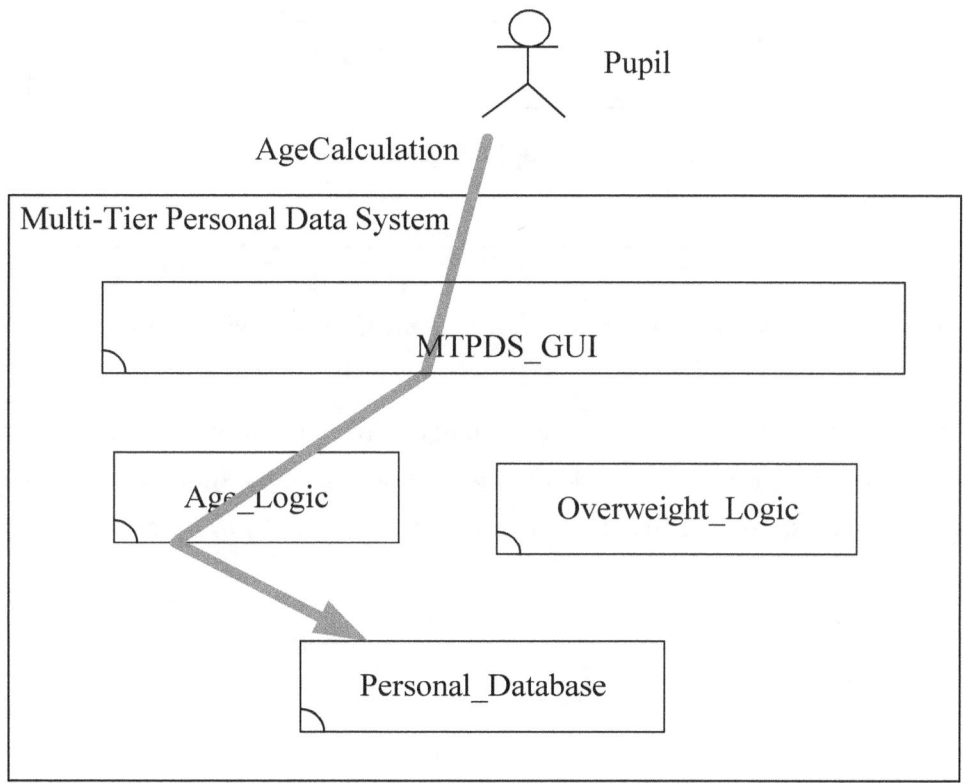

Figure 9-2   All Components, Actors, and the *AgeCalculation* Behavior

Adding the *OverweightCalculation* behavior to Figure 9-2, we then obtain the graphical representation shown in Figure 9-3. In this Figure, the *OverweightCalculation* behavior indicates that actor *Pupil* interacts with the *MTPDS_GUI* component first, then component *MTPDS_GUI* interacts with the

Overweight_Logic component later, then component *Overweight_Logic* interacts with the *Personal_Database* component finally.

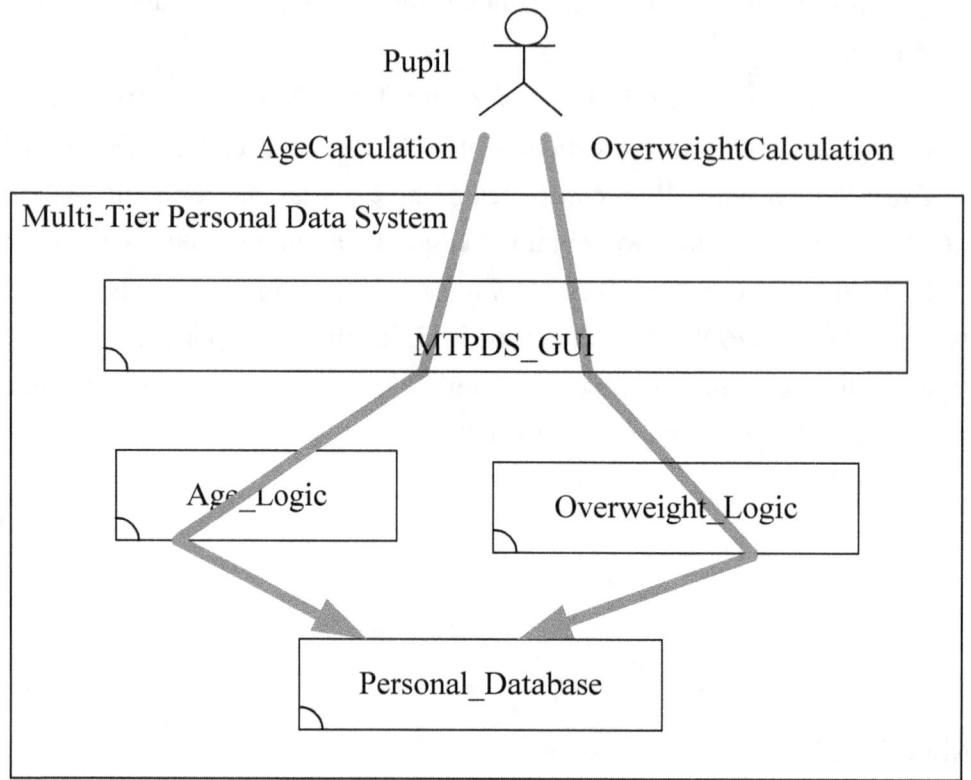

Figure 9-3   Adding the *OverweightCalculation* Behavior to Figure 9-2

After finishing Figure 8-3, we actually have accomplished all the works needed to draw an entire SBCD of *Multi-Tier Personal Data System*. As a matter of fact, Figure 6-3 is exactly the SBCD of *Multi-Tier Personal Data System*.

Chapter 10: Interaction Flow Diagram

Systems theory 2.0 (Architectural theory) uses an interaction flow diagram (IFD) to define each individual behavior of the overall behavior of a system. IFD is the sixth fundamental diagram to achieve structure-behavior coalescence.

10-1 Individual Behavior Represented by Interaction Flow Diagram

The overall behavior of a system consists of many individual behaviors. Each individual behavior represents an execution path. An IFD is utilized to define such an individual behavior.

Figure 10-1 demonstrates that the *Convenience Store's Get 2nd 50% off Sales Promotion System* has two behaviors; thus, it has two IFDs.

System	IFD
Convenience Store's Get 2nd 50% off Sales Promotion System	Advertising
	Get 2nd 50% off

Figure 10-1 Convenience Store's Get 2nd 50% off Sales Promotion System has two IFDs

Figure 10-2 demonstrates that the *Department Store's Car Sweepstakes Sales Promotion System* has three behaviors; thus, it has three IFDs.

System	IFD
Department Store's Car Sweepstakes Sales Promotion System	Get_Sweepstake_Number
	Draw_Out_the_Winners_List
	Collect_the_Winning_Car

Figure 10-2   Department Store's Car Sweepstakes Sales Promotion System has three IFDs

10-2 Drawing the Interaction Flow Diagrams

Let us now explain the usage of interaction flow diagram (IFD) by drawing an IFD step by step. Figure 10-3 demonstrates an IFD of the *AgeCalculation* behavior. The X-axis direction is from the left side to right side and the Y-axis direction is from the above to the below. Inside an IFD, there are four elements: a) external environment's actor, b) components, c) interactions and d) input/output parameters. Participants of the interaction, such as the external environment's actor and each component, are laid aside along the X-axis direction on the top of the diagram. The external environment's actor which initiates the sequential interactions is always placed on the most left side of the X-axis. Then, interactions among the external environment's actor and components successively in turn decorate along the Y-axis direction. The first interaction is placed on the top of the Y-axis position. The last interaction is placed on the bottom of the Y-axis position. Each interaction may carry several input and/or output parameters.

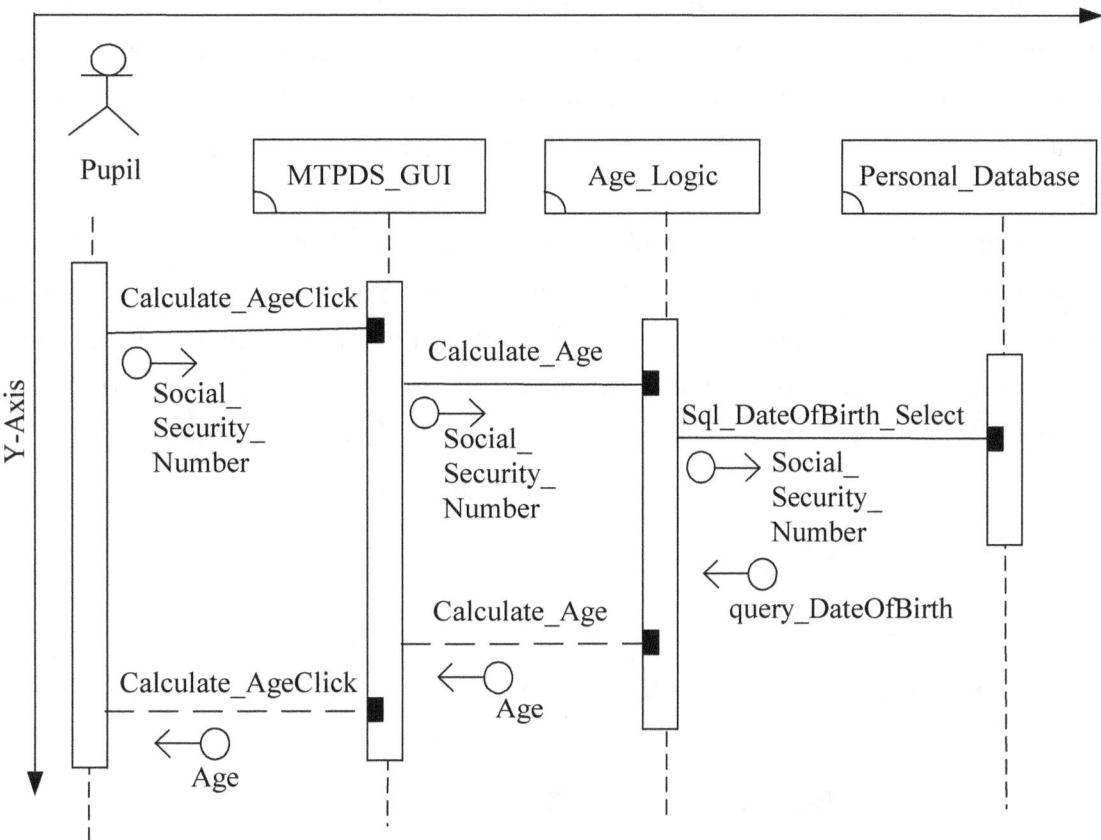

Figure 10-3 IFD of the *AgeCalculation* Behavior

In Figure 10-3, *Pupil* is an external environment's actor. *MTPDS_GUI*, *Age_Logic* and *Personal_Database* are components. *Calculate_AgeClick* is an operation provided by the *MTPDS_GUI* component, carrying the *Social_Security_Number* input parameter and *Age* output parameters. *Calculate_Age* is an operation provided by the *Age_Logic* component, carrying the *Social_Security_Number* input parameter and *Age* output parameter. *Sql_DateOfBirth_Select* is an operation provided by the component *Personal_Database*, carrying the *Social_Security_Number* input parameter and *query_DateOfBirth* output parameter.

The execution path of Figure 10-3 is as follows. First, actor *Pupil* interacts with the *MTPDS_GUI* component through the *Calculate_AgeClick* operation call interaction, carrying the *Social_Security_Number* input parameter. Next, component *MTPDS_GUI* interacts with the *Age_Logic* component through the *Calculate_Age* operation call interaction, carrying the *Social_Security_Number* input parameter. Continuingly, component *Age_Logic* interacts with the *Personal_Database* component through the *Sql_DateOfBirth_Select* operation call interaction, carrying the *Social_Security_Number* input parameter and the *query_DateOfBirth* output parameter. Repeatedly, component *MTPDS_GUI* interacts with the *Age_Logic* component through the *Calculate_Age* operation return interaction, carrying the *Age* output parameter. Finally, actor *Pupil* interacts with the *MTPDS_GUI* component through the *Calculate_AgeClick* operation return interaction, carrying the *Age* output parameter.

For each interaction, the solid line stands for operation call while the dashed line stands for operation return. The operation call and operation return interactions, if using the same operation name, belong to the identical operation. Figure 10-4 exhibits two interactions (operation call interaction and operation return interaction) having the identical "*Request*" operation.

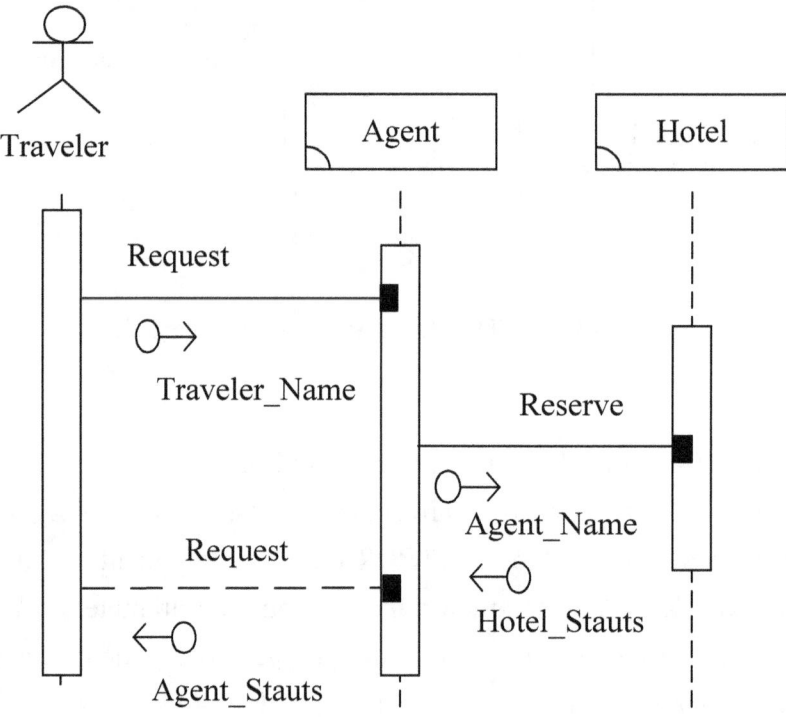

Figure 10-4   Two Interactions Have the Identical Operation

The execution path of Figure 10-4 is as follows. First, external environment's actor *Traveler* interacts with the *Agent* component through the *Request* operation call interaction, carrying the *Traveler_Name* input parameter. Next, component *Agent* interacts with the *Hotel* component through the *Reserve* operation call interaction, carrying the *Agent_Name* input parameter and *Hotel_Stauts* output parameter. Finally, external environment's actor *Traveler* interacts with the *Agent* component through the *Request* operation return interaction, carrying the *Agent_Stauts* output parameter.

An interaction flow diagram may contain a conditional expression. Figure 10-5 shows such an example which has the following execution path. First, external environment's actor *Employee* interacts with the *Computer* component through the *Open* operation call interaction, carrying the *Task_No* input parameter. Next, if the *var_1 < 4 & var_2 > 7* condition is true then component *Computer* shall interact with the *Skype* component through the *Op_1* operation call interaction and component *Skype* shall interact with the *Earphone* component through the *Op_4* operation call interaction, carrying the *Skype_Earphone* output parameter; else if the *var_3 = 99* condition is true then component *Computer* shall interact with the *Skype* component through the *Op_2* operation call interaction and component *Skype* shall interact with the *Speaker* component through the *Op_5* operation call interaction, carrying the *Skype_Speaker* output parameter; else component *Computer* shall interact with the *Youtube* component through the *Op_3* operation call interaction and component *Youtube* shall interact with the *Speaker* component through the *Op_6* operation call interaction, carrying the *Youtube_Speaker* output parameter. Continuingly, if the *var_1 < 4 & var_2 > 7* condition is true then component *Computer* shall interact with the *Skype* component through the *Op_1* operation return interaction, carrying the *Status_1* output parameter; else if the *var_3 = 99* condition is true then component *Computer* shall interact with the *Skype* component through the *Op_2* operation return interaction, carrying the *Status_2* output parameter; else component *Computer* shall interact with the *Youtube* component through the *Op_3* operation return interaction, carrying the *Status_3* output parameter. Finally, external environment's actor *Employee* interacts with the *Computer* component through the *Open* operation return interaction, carrying the *Status* output parameter.

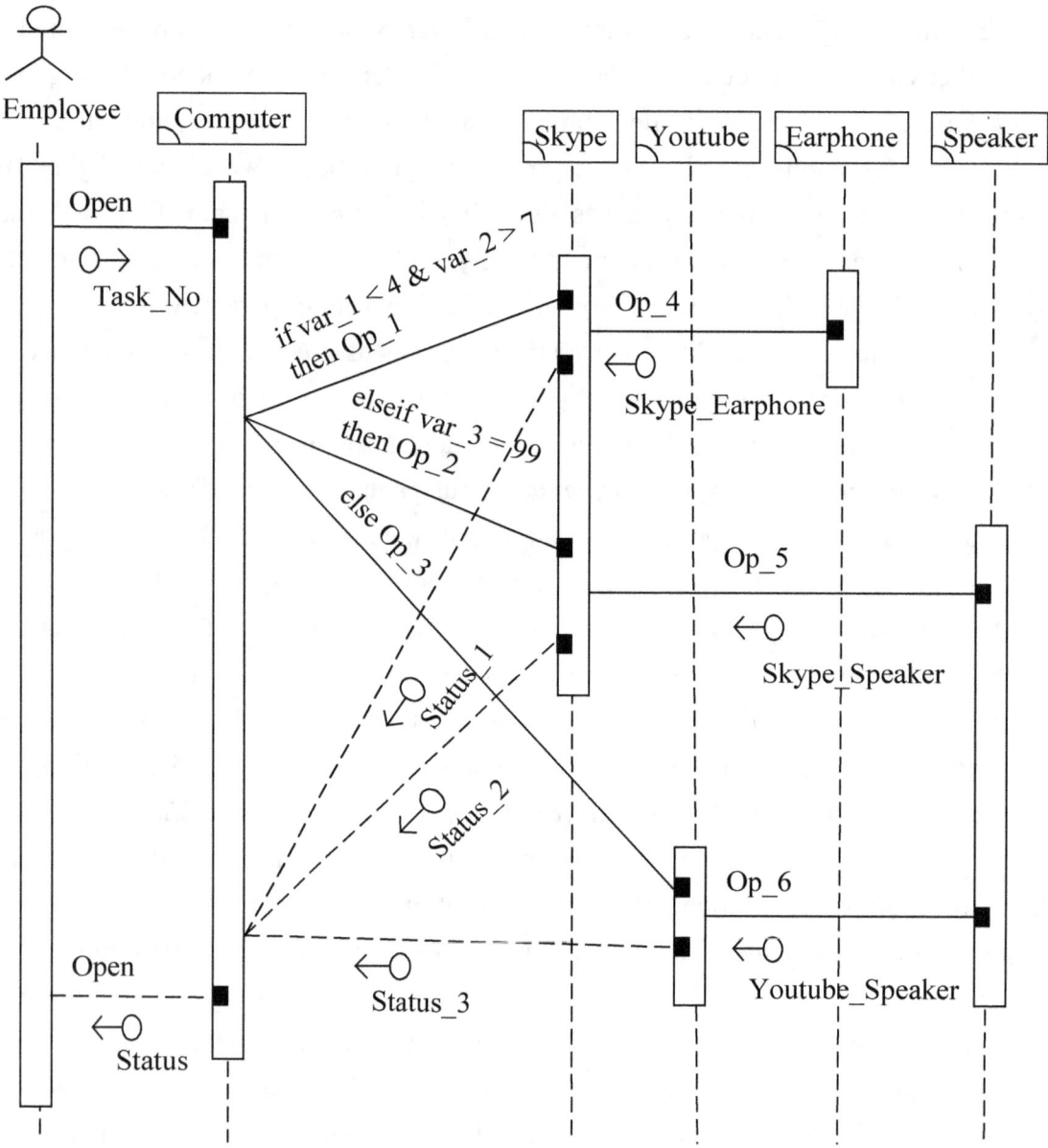

Figure 10-5   Conditional Expression

Several Boolean conditions are shown in Figure 10-5. They are "*var_1 < 4 & var_2 > 7*" and "*var_3 = 99*". Variables, such as *var_1*, *var_2* and *var_3*, appearing in the Boolean condition can be local or global variables.

PART III: CASE STUDIES

Chapter 11: Convenience Store's Get 2nd 50% off Sales Promotion Plan

In order to attract customers to buy, a convenience store may find many ways to do so. The easiest one is to give discounts. Because of human nature, coupled with the hot summer weather, the customers see the ad saying a cold drink at 50% off, they may have a great desire to buy it. This inspires the idea of a convenience store's get 2nd 50% off sales promotion plan.

In this chapter, we will follow: (01) Architecture-Oriented Convenience Store's Get 2nd 50% off Sales Promotion Planning Chart and (02) Writing Down an Architecture-Oriented Convenience Store's Get 2nd 50% off Sales Promotion Plan, to accomplish this plan.

11-1 Architecture-Oriented Convenience Store's Get 2nd 50% off Sales Promotion Planning Chart

First, we draw the architecture-oriented convenience store's get 2nd 50% off sales promotion planning chart, shown in Figure 11-1. The architecture-oriented convenience store's get 2nd 50% off sales promotion planning chart, like a mandala, can be interpreted as gradually extending outward from the innermost ring, can also be interpreted as an external gradually move closer to the innermost ring.

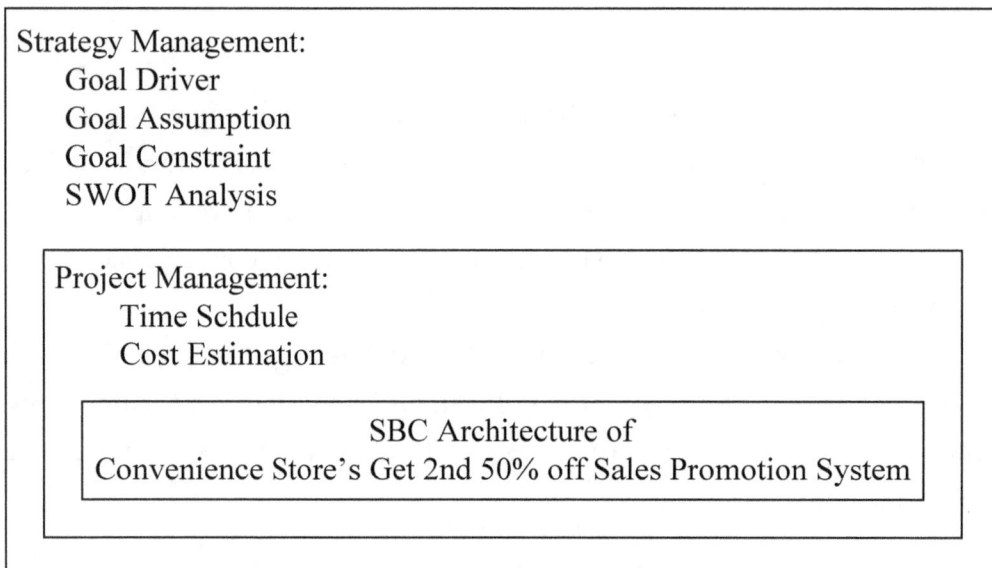

Figure 11-1   Architecture-Oriented
Convenience Store's Get 2nd 50% off Sales Promotion Planning Chart

There are three rings in the architecture-oriented convenience store's get 2nd 50% off sales promotion planning chart. The innermost ring is: (B) SBC Architecture of Convenience Store's Get 2nd 50% off Sales Promotion System; second inner ring is the project management which includes: (C1) Time Schedule, (C2) Cost Estimation; outermost ring is the strategic management which includes: (D1) Goal Drivers, (D2) Goal Assumptions, (D3) Goal Constraints and (D4) SWOT Analysis. Project management is around the "SBC architecture of convenience store's get 2nd 50% off sales promotion system". That is to say, project management is in line with the "SBC architecture of convenience store's get 2nd 50% off sales promotion system". Strategic management is around the "project management" and "SBC architecture of convenience store's get 2nd 50% off sales promotion system". That is to say, strategic management is in line with the "project management" and "SBC architecture of convenience store's get 2nd 50% off sales promotion system".

11-2 Writing Down an Architecture-Oriented Convenience Store's Get 2nd 50% off Sales Promotion Plan

With the architecture-oriented convenience store's get 2nd 50% off sales promotion planning chart, we are able to write down an architecture-oriented convenience store's get 2nd 50% off sales promotion plan.

Basically, the architecture-oriented convenience store's get 2nd 50% off sales promotion plan follows: (A01) Title and Cover, (A02) Contents, (A03) Planning Team Members, (A04) Planning Purposes, (B) Planning Objectives (SBC Architecture of Convenience Store's Get 2nd 50% off Sales Promotion System), (C01) Time Schedule, (C02) Cost Estimation, (D01) Goal Drivers, (D02) Goal Assumptions, (D03) Goal Constraints and (D04) SWOT Analysis, as shown in Figure 11-2.

Convenience Store's Get 2nd 50% off Sales Promotion Plan

(Page 1 / 10)

Title and Cover

Get 2nd 50% off

Sales Promotion Plan

Cold Drink 50% Off

July 12, 2014

Figure 11-2   Architecture-Oriented Convenience Store's Get 2nd 50% off Sales Promotion Plan

---

Convenience Store's Get 2nd 50% off Sales Promotion Plan

(Page 2 / 10)

Table of Contents

Table of Contents
Planning Team Members
Planning Purposes
Planning Objectives
Time Schedule
Cost Estimation
Goal Drivers
Goal Assumptions
Goal Constraints
SWOT Analysis

Planning Team Members

Back office staff :
    James Kurt (head office Planning Department)
    Mary Bryant (Headquarters Advertising Department)
    Lee Hull (Headquarters Designer)
Field staff :
    Arthur Chen (Advertising Company President)
    Timothy Kaplan (Advertising Photographer)
    Shan Hutchison (Advertising Company Contact Person)

Planning Purposes

    Summer is coming, getting the 2nd cold drink buy 50% off should have some drive to the sales promotion effect. This is the main purpose of this planning.

Figure 11-2   Architecture-Oriented Convenience Store's Get 2nd 50% off Sales Promotion Plan

Convenience Store's Get 2nd 50% off Sales Promotion Plan

(Page 3 / 10)

Planning Objectives
(SBC Architecture of Convenience Store's Get 2nd 50% off Sales Promotion System)

The main objective of this planning is "get 2nd 50% off sales promotion for a convenience store." As shown in the below figures, we use the SBC-ADL to describe the objective of this planning.

Architecture Hierarchy Diagram

We use an architecture hierarchy diagram (AHD) to define the multi-level composition and decomposition of the "Convenience Store's Get 2nd 50% off Sales Promotion System." As shown in the following figure, "Convenience Store's Get 2nd 50% off Sales Promotion System" is composed of "Clerk" and "Subsystem_1"; "Subsystem_1" is composed of "Advertising_Board."

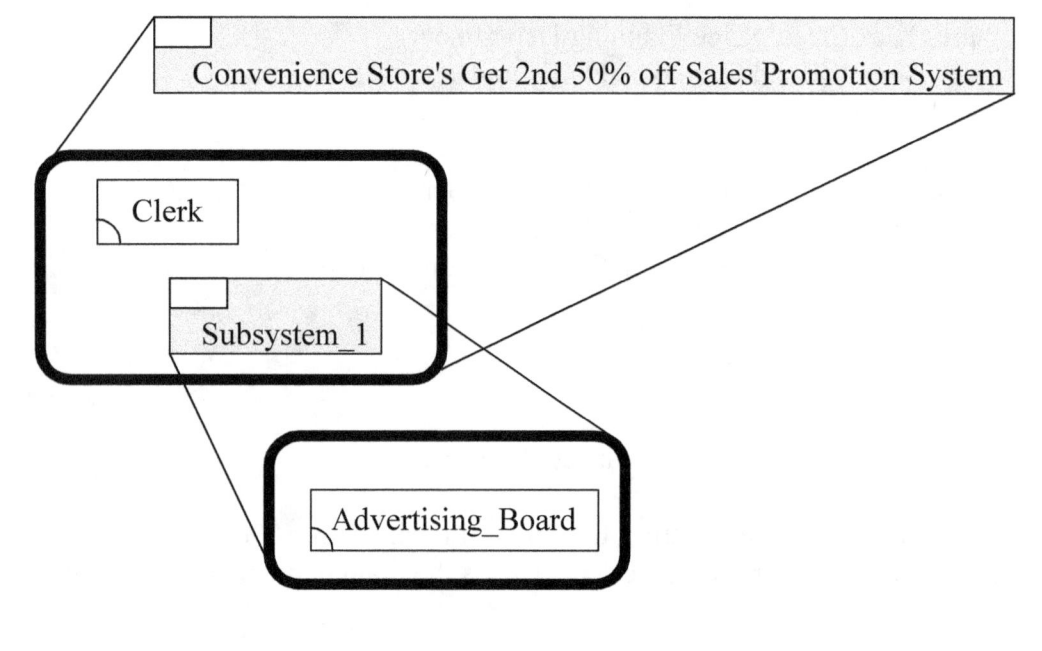

Figure 11-2 Architecture-Oriented Convenience Store's Get 2nd 50% off Sales Promotion Plan

Convenience Store's Get 2nd 50% off Sales Promotion Plan

(Page 4 / 10)

Framework Diagram

    We use a framework diagram (FD) to define the multi-layer composition and decomposition of the "Convenience Store's Get 2nd 50% off Sales Promotion System" as shown below. In the figure, Business Layer contains the "Clerk" component; Application Layer contains the "Advertising_Board" component.

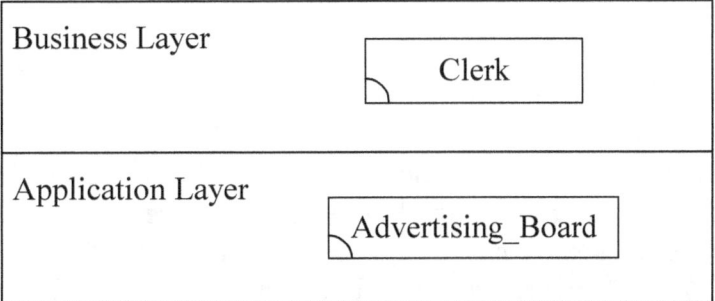

Component Operation Diagram

    We use a component operation diagram (COD) to define the operations of all components of the "Convenience Store's Get 2nd 50% off Sales Promotion System" as shown below. In the figure, component "Advertising_Board" has one operation: "Watch"; component "Clerk" has two operations: "Buy the 1st Goods" and "Buy the 2nd Goods."

Figure 11-2   Architecture-Oriented Convenience Store's Get 2nd 50% off Sales Promotion Plan

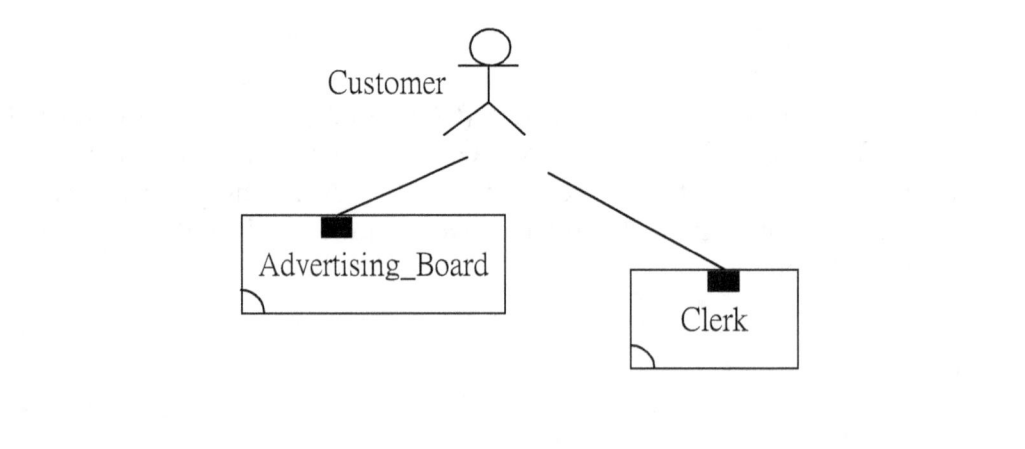

Component Connection Diagram

We use a component connection diagram (CCD) to define the connections among components and actors of the "Convenience Store's Get 2nd 50% off Sales Promotion System" as shown below. In the figure, actor "Customer" has one connection with the "Advertising_Board" component; actor "Customer" has one connection with the "Clerk" component.

Figure 11-2 Architecture-Oriented Convenience Store's Get 2nd 50% off Sales Promotion Plan

Convenience Store's Get 2nd 50% off Sales Promotion Plan

(Page 6 / 10)

Structure-Behavior Coalescence Diagram

We use a structure-behavior coalescence diagram (SBCD) to define the structure and behavior coexisting in the "Convenience Store's Get 2nd 50% off Sales Promotion System" as shown below. In the figure, interactions among the "Customer" actor and the "Advertising_Board", "Clerk" components generate the "Advertising" and "Get 2nd 50% off" behaviors.

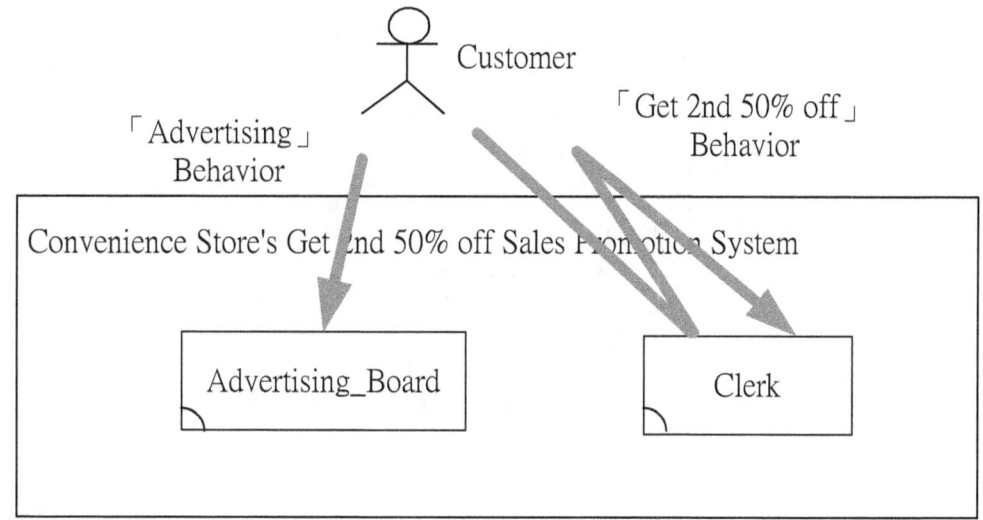

Figure 11-2 Architecture-Oriented Convenience Store's Get 2nd 50% off Sales Promotion Plan

Convenience Store's Get 2nd 50% off Sales Promotion Plan

(Page 7 / 10)

Interaction Flow Diagram

The overall behavior of the "Convenience Store's Get 2nd 50% off Sales Promotion System" includes two individual behaviors: *Advertising* and *Get 2nd 50% off.* Each individual behavior is represented by an execution path. We use an IFD to define each one of these execution paths. Below figure shows an IFD of the "Advertising" behavior. First, actor "Customer" interacts with the "Advertising_Board" component through the "Watch" operation call interaction, carrying the "Advertisement" output parameter.

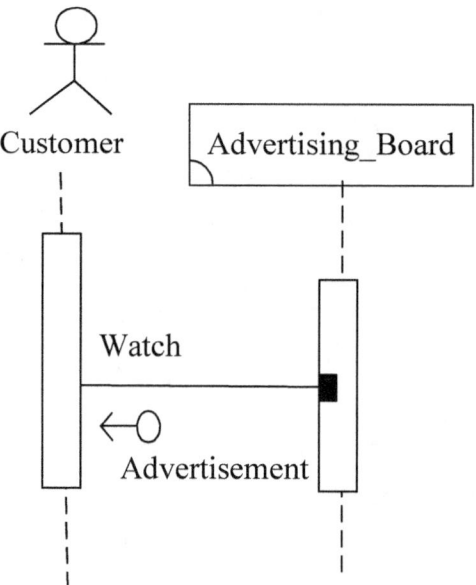

Below figure shows an IFD of the "Get 2nd 50% off" behavior. First, actor "Customer" interacts with the "Clerk" component through the "Buy the 1st Goods" operation call interaction, carrying the "Payment" input parameter and "Goods" output parameter. Last, actor "Customer" interacts with the "Clerk" component through the "Buy the 2nd Goods" operation call interaction, carrying the "50% off Payment" input parameter and "Cold Drink" output parameter.

Figure 11-2 Architecture-Oriented Convenience Store's Get 2nd 50% off Sales Promotion Plan

Convenience Store's Get 2nd 50% off Sales Promotion Plan

(Page 8 / 10)

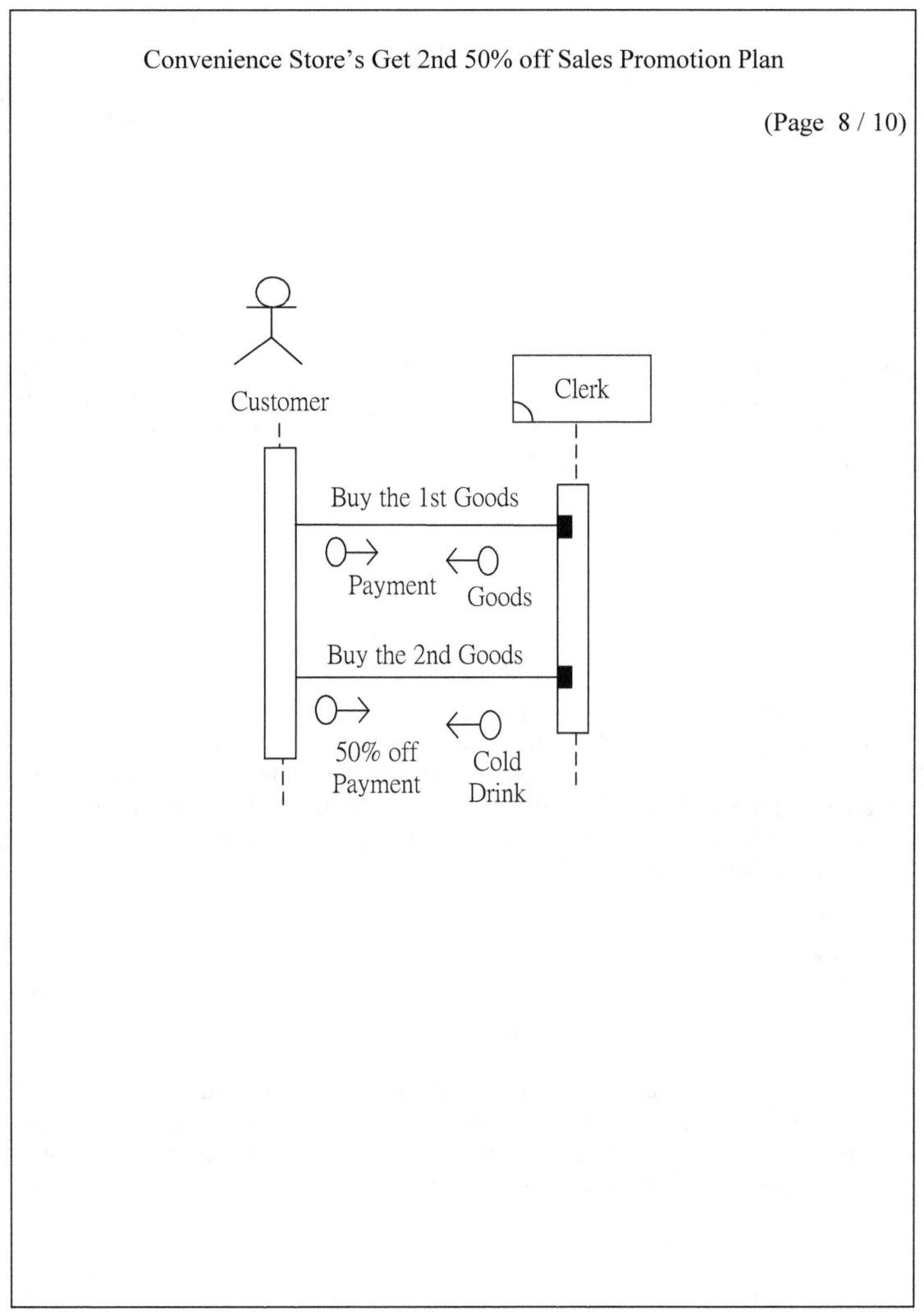

Figure 11-2 Architecture-Oriented Convenience Store's Get 2nd 50% off Sales Promotion Plan

> Convenience Store's Get 2nd 50% off Sales Promotion Plan
>
> (Page 9 / 10)
>
> Time Schedule
>
> "Convenience Store's Get 2nd 50% off Sales Promotion Plan" consists of the "Advertising_Board" and "Clerk" components. These two components must be at 1 May 2014 on the position. And the working time of these two components will begin on May 1, 2014 and end on October 31, 2014, with a time period of six months.
>
> Cost Estimation
>
> "Advertising_Board" and "Clerk" are the components in the "Convenience Store's Get 2nd 50% off Sales Promotion Plan." The development and maintenance fee of "Advertising_Board" is NT200,000 dollars. Each "Clerk" in the "Convenience Store's Get 2nd 50% off Sales Promotion Plan" gets half a year's salary of NT30,000 dollars for his (or her) extra work. If there are N stores, then the total cost will be NT(200,000 + 30,000*N)dollars.
>
> Goal Drivers
>
> Goal drivers are up from the policy considerations, the goal driver is kind of how we got to be this prompted planning. The goal drivers are: sales market downturn, and thus required a promotion; summer is coming, there will be cold drinks promotional effect; promotions from time to time it, often to promote sales.

Figure 11-2 Architecture-Oriented Convenience Store's Get 2nd 50% off Sales Promotion Plan

> Convenience Store's Get 2nd 50% off Sales Promotion Plan
>
> (Page 10 / 10)
>
> Goal Assumptions
>
> Goal assumptions are taking into account of those assumptions that have a positive impact on this planning. We assume that in the summer time, a customer has a great desire to buy if he can get the 2nd goods cold drink 50% off. This is the major goal assumption of this "Convenience Store's Get 2nd 50% off Sales Promotion Plan."
>
> Goal Constraints
>
> Goal constraints are up from the policy considerations, the goal constraints are related to those restrictions which have a negative impact on this planning. If the company is short of funding to carry out this planning, then this would become the goal constraint of this "Convenience Store's Get 2nd 50% off Sales Promotion Plan."
>
> SWOT Analysis
>
> Being a leader of convenience stores, it should be trivial to execute the planning. This is the internal strength of this company. However, kind of bulky makes it may not react fast enough to carry out the planning. This is the internal weakness of this company.

Figure 11-2   Architecture-Oriented Convenience Store's Get 2nd 50% off Sales Promotion Plan

Chapter 12: Department Store's Car Sweepstakes Sales Promotion Plan

A decent car is something everyone wants to have. A customer will be interested in buying a thousand dollars goods in a department store if he has the opportunity to get a grand new one-million-dollars car.

In this chapter, we will follow: (01) Architecture-Oriented Department Store's Car Sweepstakes Sales Promotion Planning Chart and (02) Writing Down an Architecture-Oriented Department Store's Car Sweepstakes Sales Promotion Plan, to accomplish this plan.

12-1 Architecture-Oriented Department Store's Car Sweepstakes Sales Promotion Planning Chart

First, we draw the architecture-oriented department store's car sweepstakes sales promotion planning chart, shown in Figure 12-1. The architecture-oriented department store's car sweepstakes sales promotion planning chart, like a mandala, can be interpreted as gradually extending outward from the innermost ring, can also be interpreted as an external gradually move closer to the innermost ring.

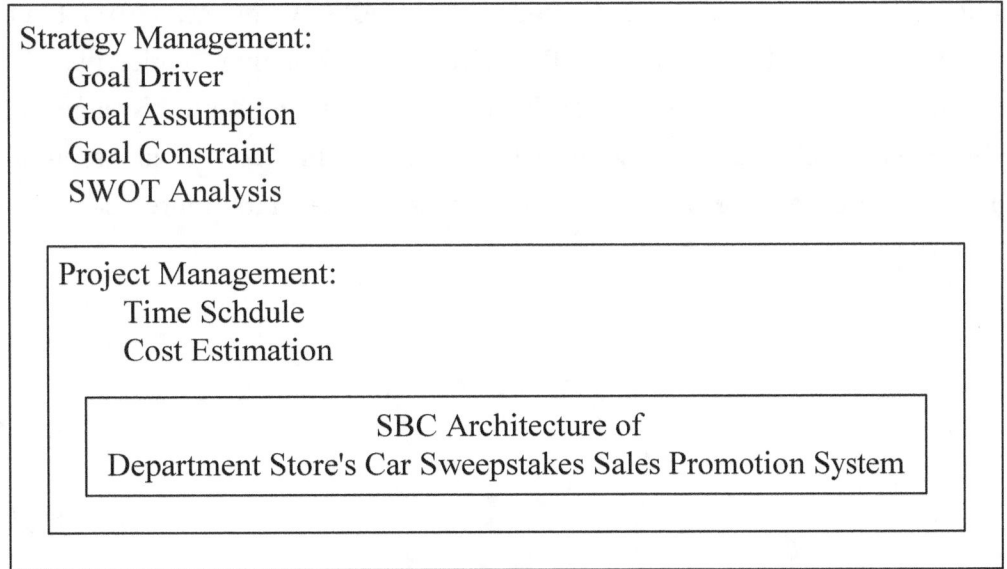

Figure 12-1 Architecture-Oriented Department Store's Car Sweepstakes Sales Promotion Planning Chart

There are three rings in the architecture-oriented department store's car sweepstakes sales promotion planning chart. The innermost ring is: (B) SBC Architecture of Department Store's Car Sweepstakes Sales Promotion System; second inner ring is the project management which includes: (C1) Time Schedule, (C2) Cost Estimation; outermost ring is the strategic management which includes: (D1) Goal Drivers, (D2) Goal Assumptions, (D3) Goal Constraints and (D4) SWOT Analysis. Project management is around the "SBC architecture of department store's car sweepstakes sales promotion system". That is to say, project management is in line with the "SBC architecture of department store's car sweepstakes sales promotion system". Strategic management is around the "project management" and "SBC architecture of department store's car sweepstakes sales promotion system". That is to say, strategic management is in line with the "project management" and "SBC architecture of department store's car sweepstakes sales promotion system".

12-2 Writing Down an Architecture-Oriented Department Store's Car Sweepstakes Sales Promotion Plan

With the architecture-oriented department store's car sweepstakes sales promotion planning chart, we are able to write down an architecture-oriented department store's car sweepstakes sales promotion plan.

Basically, the architecture-oriented department store's car sweepstakes sales promotion plan follows: (A01) Title and Cover, (A02) Contents, (A03) Planning Team Members, (A04) Planning Purposes, (B) Planning Objectives (SBC Architecture of Department Store's Car Sweepstakes Sales Promotion System), (C01) Time Schedule, (C02) Cost Estimation, (D01) Goal Drivers, (D02) Goal Assumptions, (D03) Goal Constraints and (D04) SWOT Analysis, as shown in Figure 12-2.

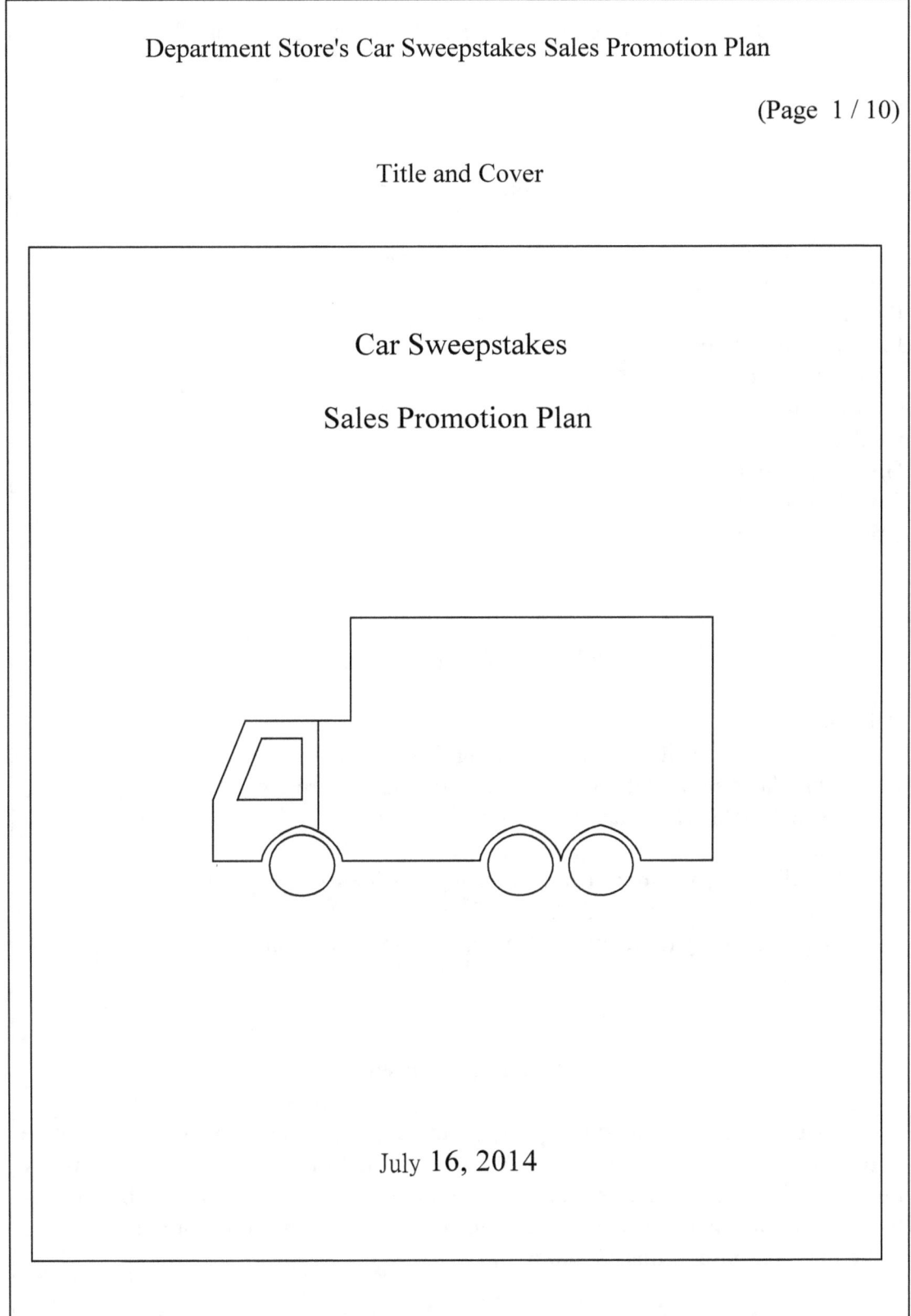

Figure 12-2 Architecture-Oriented Department Store's Car Sweepstakes Sales Promotion Plan

Department Store's Car Sweepstakes Sales Promotion Plan

(Page 2 / 10)

Table of Contents

Table of Contents
Planning Team Members
Planning Purposes
Planning Objectives
Time Schedule
Cost Estimation
Goal Drivers
Goal Assumptions
Goal Constraints
SWOT Analysis

Planning Team Members

Back office staff :
     James Walker (head office Planning Department)
     Douglas Ashton (Headquarters Advertising Department)
     Hull Arnold (Headquarters Designer)
Field staff :
     William Chen (Advertising Company President)
     Timothy McCorkle (Advertising Photographer)
     Khan Banathy (Advertising Company Contact Person)

Planning Purposes

    Being the only department store in the city, no other company can compete with it in this sales promotion plan. We assume that in a period of approximately three months promotional period, customers will have a great desire to buy a one-thousand-dollars goods if they have a chance to get a one-million-dollars car. This is the main purpose of this planning.

Figure 12-2   Architecture-Oriented Department Store's Car Sweepstakes Sales Promotion Plan

Department Store's Car Sweepstakes Sales Promotion Plan

(Page 3 / 10)

Planning Objectives
(SBC Architecture of Department Store's Car Sweepstakes Sales Promotion System)

The main objective of this planning is "car sweepstakes sales promotion for a department store." As shown in the below figures, we use the SBC-ADL to describe the objective of this planning.

Architecture Hierarchy Diagram

We use the architecture hierarchy diagram (AHD) to define the multi-level composition and decomposition of the "Department Store's Car Sweepstakes Sales Promotion System." As shown in the following figure, "Department Store's Car Sweepstakes Sales Promotion System" is composed of "Clerk," "Sweepstake Host," "General Manager,"and "Subsystem_1"; "Subsystem_1" is composed of "Sweepstake _GUI."

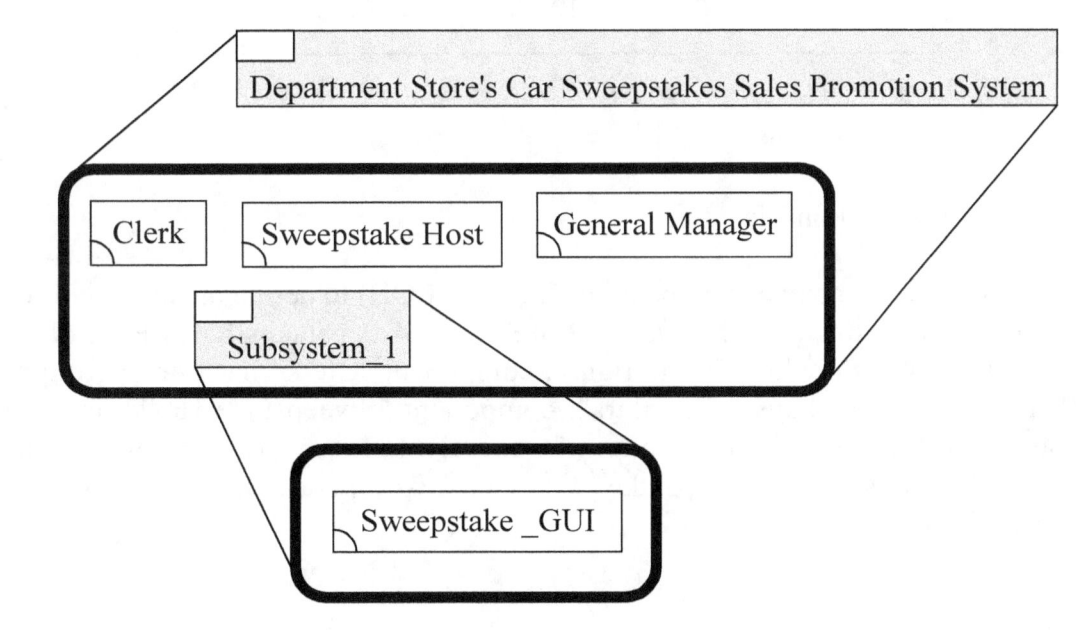

Figure 12-2 Architecture-Oriented Department Store's Car Sweepstakes Sales Promotion Plan

Department Store's Car Sweepstakes Sales Promotion Plan

(Page 4 / 10)

Framework Diagram

We use the framework diagram (FD) to define the multi-layer composition and decomposition of the "Department Store's Car Sweepstakes Sales Promotion System" as shown below. In the figure, Business Layer contains the components "Clerk,""Sweepstake Host,"and "General Manager,"; Application Layer contains the component "Sweepstake _GUI."

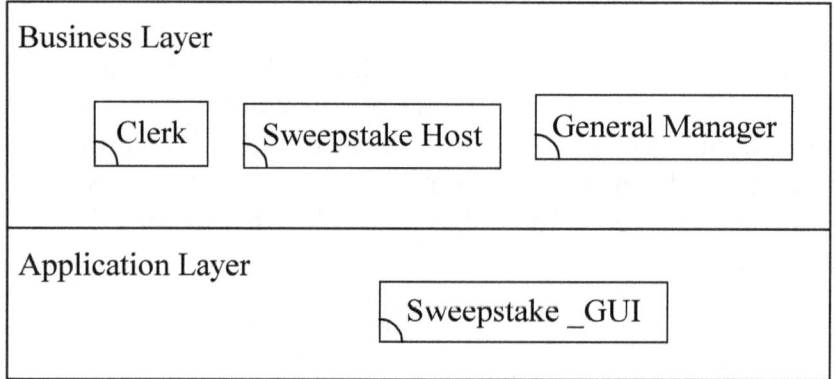

Component Operation Diagram

We use the component operation diagram (COD) to define the operations of all components of the "Department Store's Car Sweepstakes Sales Promotion System" as shown below. In the figure, component "Clerk" has one operation: "Buy More Than Thousand Dollars"; component "Sweepstake Host" has one operation: "Draw Out"; component "General Manager" has one operation: "Award"; component "Sweepstake _GUI" has two operations: "Register" and "Lucky Draw."

Figure 12-2 Architecture-Oriented Department Store's Car Sweepstakes Sales Promotion Plan

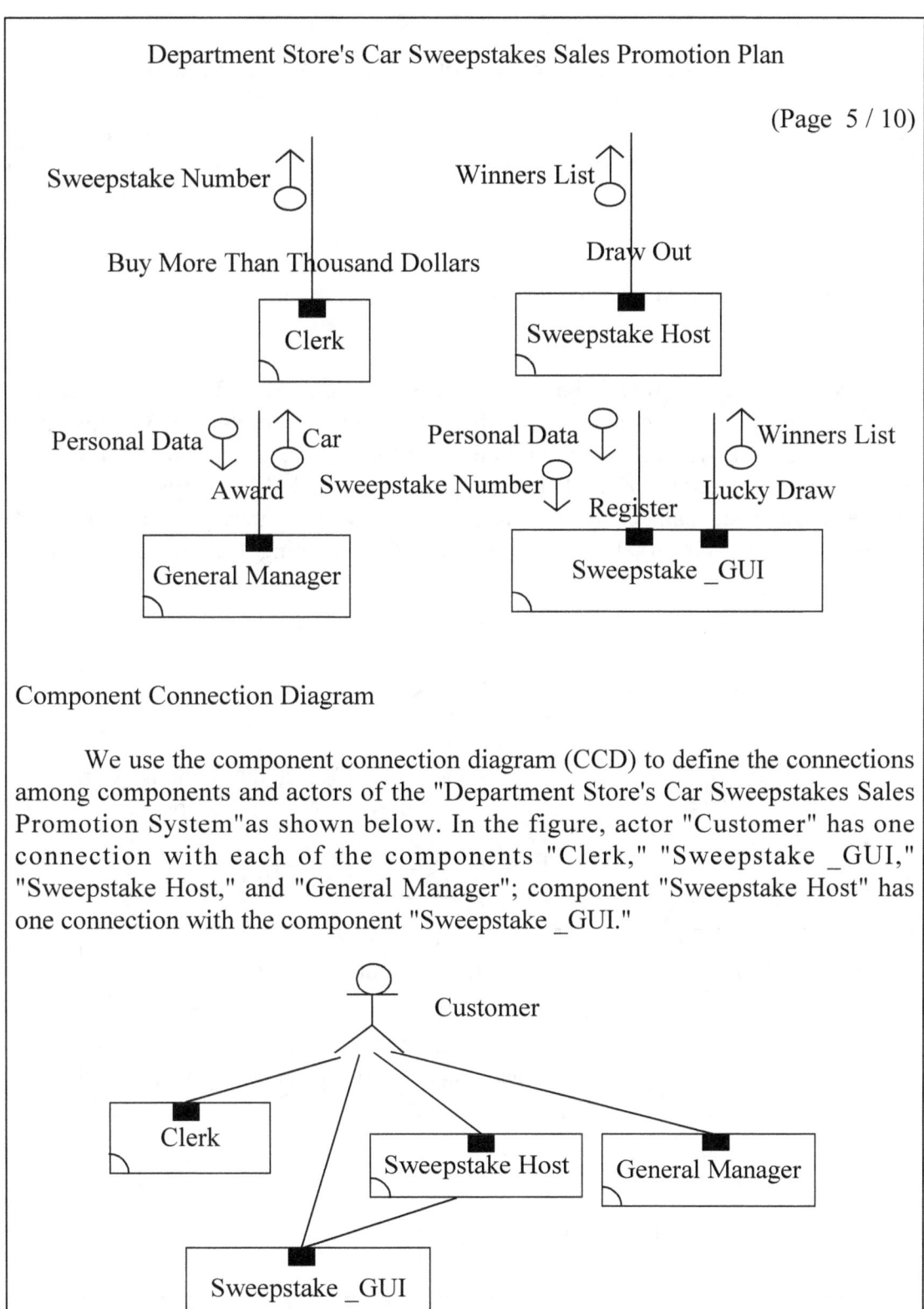

Component Connection Diagram

We use the component connection diagram (CCD) to define the connections among components and actors of the "Department Store's Car Sweepstakes Sales Promotion System" as shown below. In the figure, actor "Customer" has one connection with each of the components "Clerk," "Sweepstake_GUI," "Sweepstake Host," and "General Manager"; component "Sweepstake Host" has one connection with the component "Sweepstake_GUI."

Figure 12-2 Architecture-Oriented Department Store's Car Sweepstakes Sales Promotion Plan

Department Store's Car Sweepstakes Sales Promotion Plan

(Page 6 / 10)

Structure-Behavior Coalescence Diagram

We use the structure-behavior coalescence diagram (SBCD) to define the structure and behavior coexisting in the "Department Store's Car Sweepstakes Sales Promotion System" as shown below. In the figure, interactions among the external actor "Customer" and the components "Clerk," "Sweepstake _GUI," "Sweepstake Host," and "General Manager" generate "Get_Sweepstake_ Number," "Draw_Out_the_ Winners_List," and "Collect_the_Winning_Car" three behaviors.

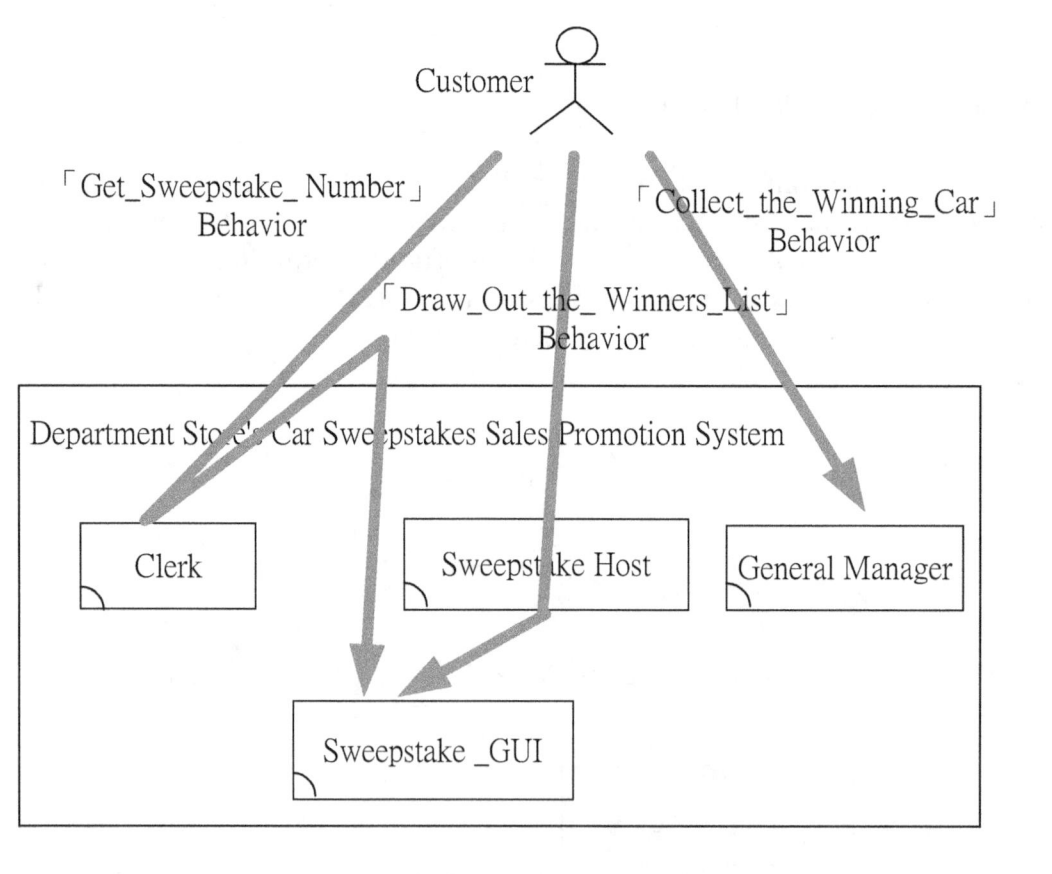

Figure 12-2   Architecture-Oriented Department Store's Car Sweepstakes Sales Promotion Plan

Department Store's Car Sweepstakes Sales Promotion Plan

(Page 7 / 10)

Interaction Flow Diagram

The overall behavior of the "Department Store's Car Sweepstakes Sales Promotion System" includes three individual behaviors: "Get_Sweepstake_ Number," "Draw_Out_the_ Winners_List," and "Collect_the_Winning_Car." Each individual behavior is represented by an execution path. We use an IFD to define each one of these execution paths.

Below figure shows the IFD of the behavior "Get_Sweepstake_ Number." First, actor "Customer" interacts with the component "Clerk" through the operation call interaction "Buy More Than Thousand Dollars," carrying the output parameter "Sweepstake Number." Last, actor "Customer" interacts with the component "Sweepstake _GUI" through the operation call interaction "Register," carrying the input parameters "Personal Data" and "Sweepstake Number."

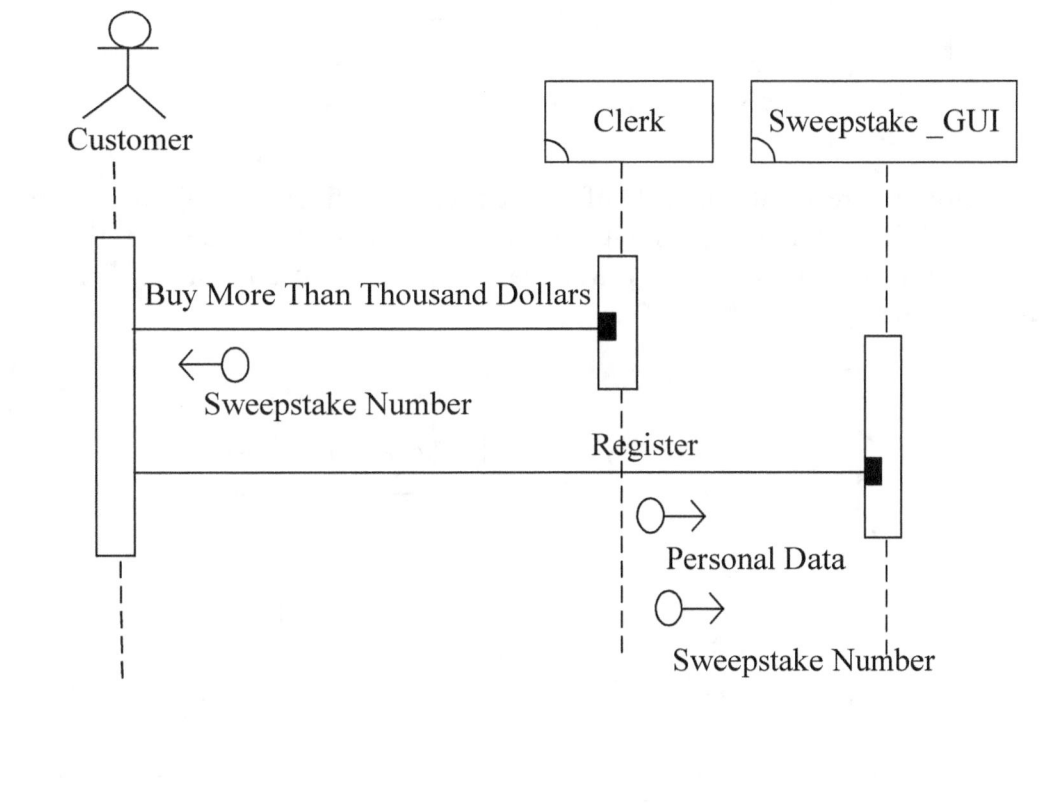

Figure 12-2   Architecture-Oriented Department Store's Car Sweepstakes Sales Promotion Plan

Department Store's Car Sweepstakes Sales Promotion Plan

(Page 8 / 10)

Below figure shows the IFD of the behavior "Draw_Out_the_ Winners_List." First, actor "Customer" interacts with the component "Sweepstake Host" through the operation call interaction "Draw Out." Next, comonent "Sweepstake Host" interacts with the component "Sweepstake _GUI" through the operation call interaction "Lucky Draw," carrying the output parameter "Winners List." Last, actor "Customer" interacts with the component "Sweepstake Host" through the operation return interaction "Draw Out," carrying the output parameter "Winners List."

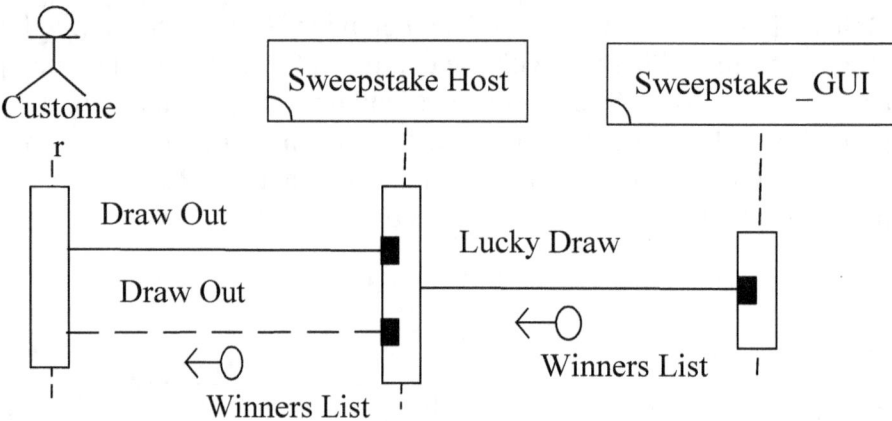

Below figure shows the IFD of the behavior "Collect_the_Winning_Car." First, actor "Customer" interacts with the component "General Manager" through the operation call interaction "Award," carrying the input parameter "Personal Data" and output parameter "Car."

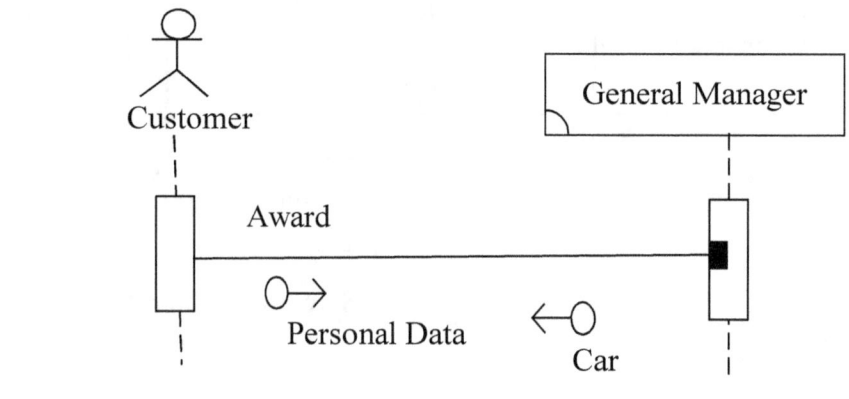

Figure 12-2   Architecture-Oriented Department Store's Car Sweepstakes Sales Promotion Plan

> Department Store's Car Sweepstakes Sales Promotion Plan
>
> (Page 9 / 10)
>
> Time Schedule
>
> "Department Store's Car Sweepstakes Sales Promotion Plan" consists of "Clerk," "Sweepstake Host," "General Manager," and "Sweepstake _GUI" four components.
> The "Clerk" component will be on the position at January 1, 2014 and off the position on March 31, 2014.
> The "Sweepstake Host" component will be on the position at on April 1, 2014 at 10:00 AM and off the position on April 1, 2014 at 11:00 AM.
> The "General Manager" component will be on the position at on April 2, 2014 at 10:00 AM and off the position on April 2, 2014 at 11:00 AM.
> The "Sweepstake _GUI" component will be on the position at January 1, 2014 and off the position on April 1, 2014.
>
> Cost Estimation
>
> "Clerk," "Sweepstake Host," "General Manager," and "Sweepstake _GUI" are the four components in the "Department Store's Car Sweepstakes Sales Promotion Plan." The "Clerk" in the "Department Store's Car Sweepstakes Sales Promotion Plan" gets 3 months' salary of NT15,000 dollars for his extra work. The "Sweepstake Host" gets NT3,000 dollars for his 1 hour work. The "General Manager," gets NT5,000 dollars for his 1 hour work. The development and maintenance fee of "Sweepstake _GUI" is NT150,000 dollars. If there are N stores, then the total cost will be (15,000 + 3,000, 5,000 + 150,000)= 173,000 NTdollars. In addition to the 1 million NT dollars of the car sweepstakes, the total cost of the "Department Store's Car Sweepstakes Sales Promotion Plan" is 1,173,000 NT dollars.

Figure 12-2   Architecture-Oriented Department Store's Car Sweepstakes Sales Promotion Plan

Department Store's Car Sweepstakes Sales Promotion Plan

(Page 10 / 10)

Goal Drivers

Goal drivers are up from the policy considerations, the goal driver is kind of how we got to be this prompted planning. The goal drivers are: there are promotional effects for purchasing a one-thousand-dollars goods will have a chance to get a one-million-dollars car; promotions from time to time it, often to promote sales.

Goal Assumptions

Goal assumptions are taking into account of those assumptions that have a positive impact on this planning. We assume that in a period of approximately three months promotional period, customers will have a great desire to buy a one-thousand-dollars goods if they have a chance to a one-million-dollars car. This is the major goal assumption of this "Department Store's Car Sweepstakes Sales Promotion Plan."

Goal Constraints

Goal constraints are up from the policy considerations, the goal constraints are related to those restrictions which have a negative impact on this planning. If the company is short of funding to carry out this planning, then this would become the goal constraint of this "Department Store's Car Sweepstakes Sales Promotion Plan."

SWOT Analysis

Being the only department store in the city, no other company can compete with it in this sales promotion plan. This is the internal strength of this company. But also worried that the company has never had similar activities, staff may not be skillful in carrying out such a plan. This is the internal weakness of this company.

Figure 12-2 Architecture-Oriented Department Store's Car Sweepstakes Sales Promotion Plan

APPENDIX: SBC ARCHITECTURE DESCRIPTION LANGUAGE

(1) Architecture Hierarchy Diagram

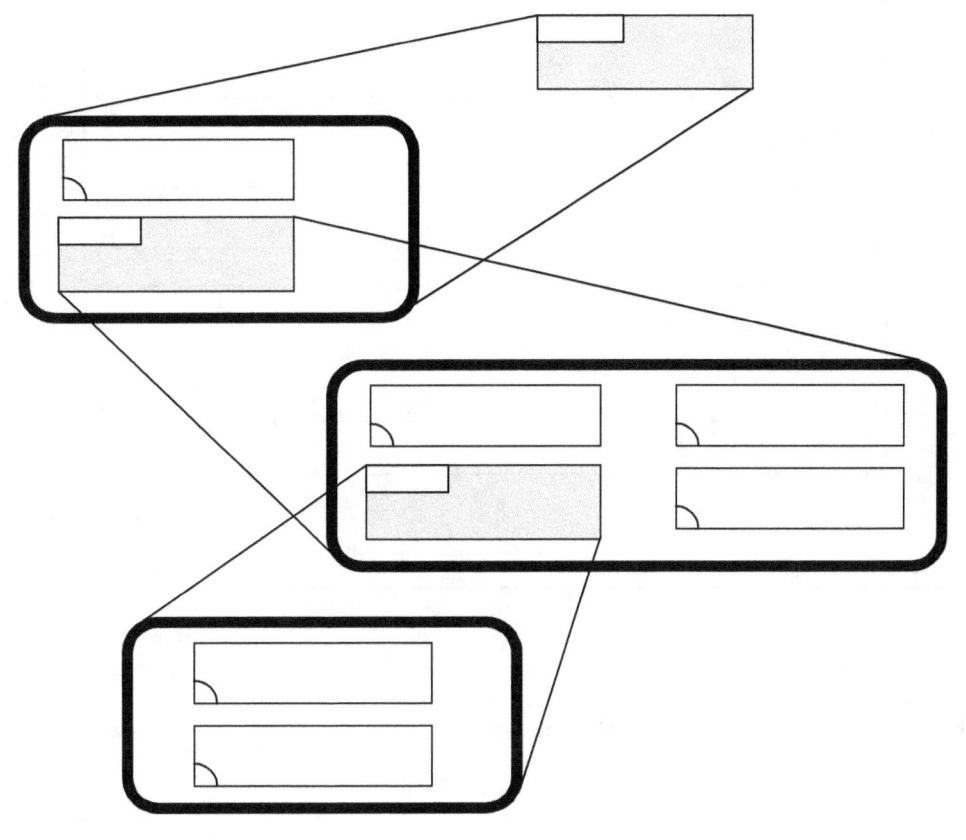

: Aggregated System

: Non-Aggregated System, Component

(2) Framework Diagram

Business Layer		
Application Layer		
Data Layer		
Technology Layer		

▱ : Component

(3) Component Operation Diagram

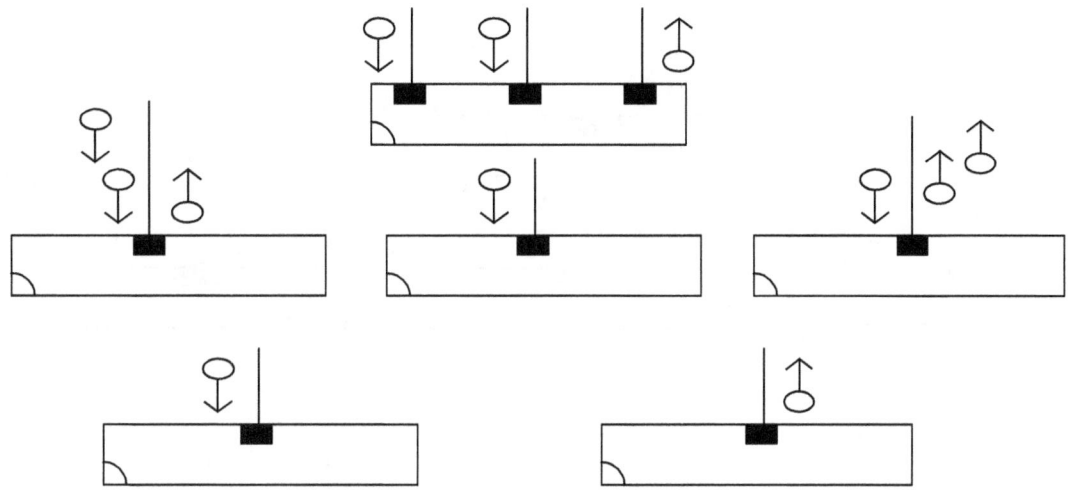

▪ (with line)	: Operation
↓ (with circle)	: Input Data
↑ (with circle)	: Output Data
▭	: Component

(4) Component Connection Diagram

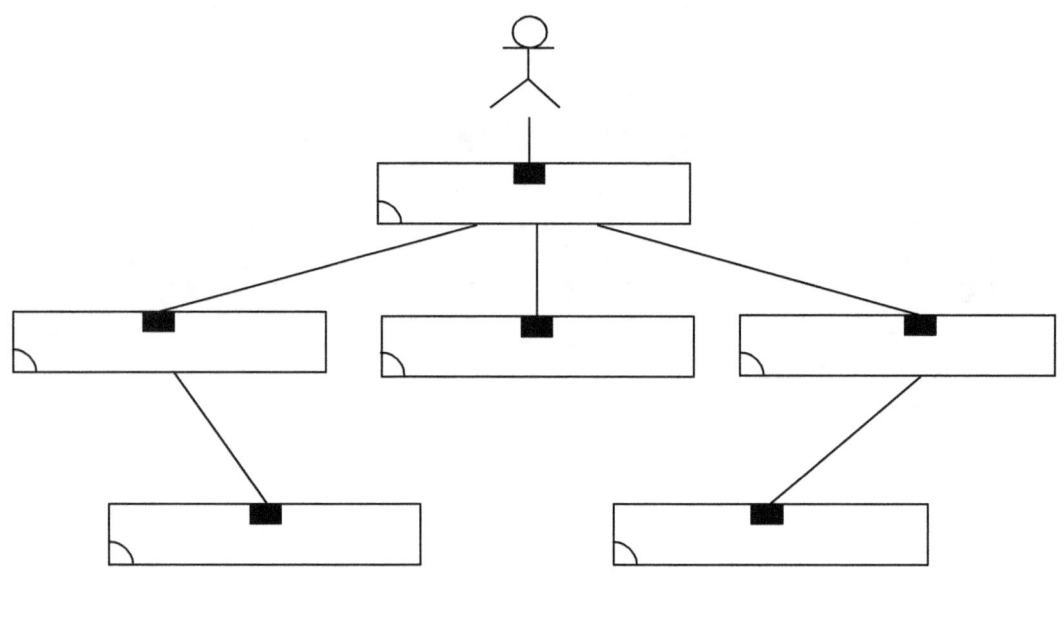

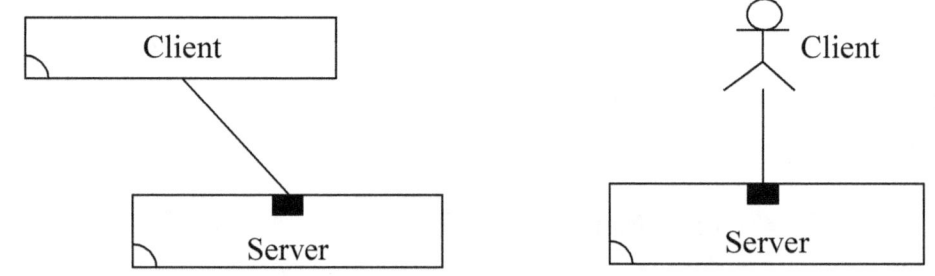

(5) Structure-Behavior Coalescence Diagram

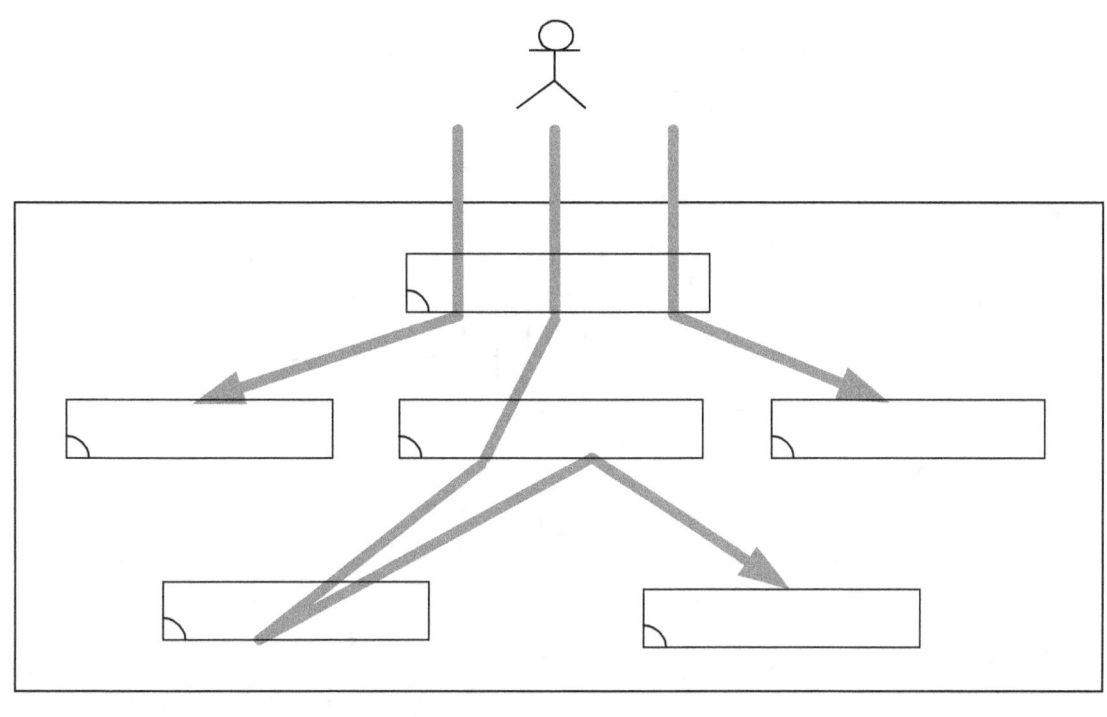

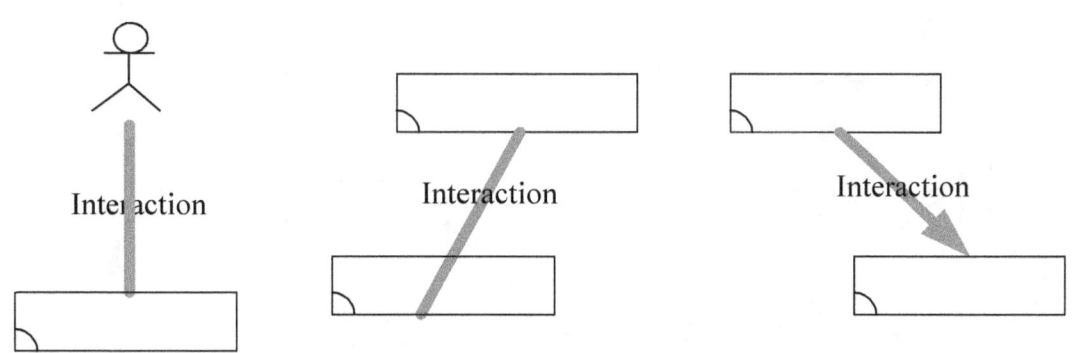

Interaction   Interaction   Interaction

(6) Interaction Flow Diagram

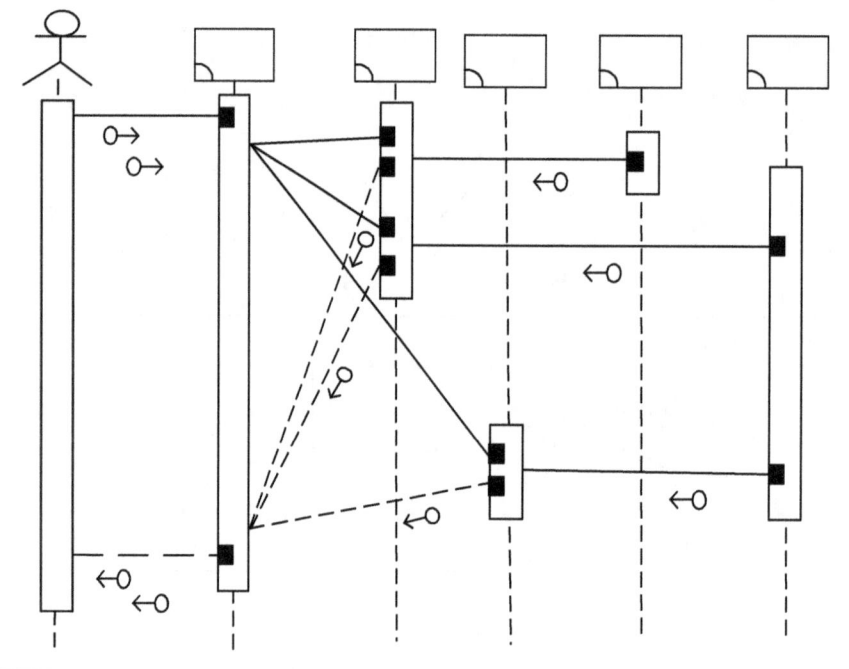

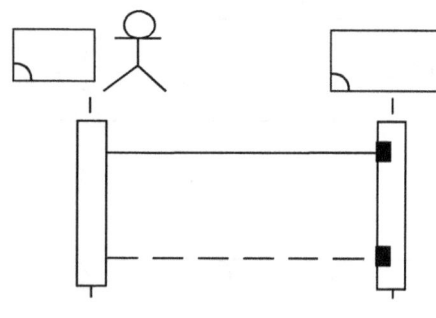

: Operation Call Interaction

: Operation Return Interaction

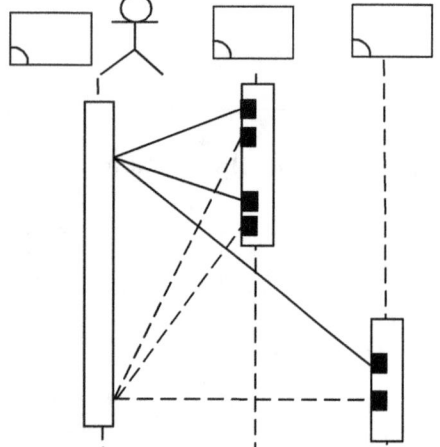

: Conditional Operation Call Interaction

: Conditional Operation Return Interaction

: Input Data

: Output Data

www.ingramcontent.com/pod-product-compliance
Lightning Source LLC
Chambersburg PA
CBHW080302180526
45167CB00006B/2643